"Like A Course in Miracles and the Abraham teachings, Expressway to Clarity empowers you to become a conscious learner. It offers simple, practical guidance for changing your mind to get to your heart and rediscover your true self, which is love."
—BOB ROSENTHAL, M.D., AUTHOR, FROM PLAGUES TO MIRACLES

Expressway to Clarity

Your Awakening Journey

AFSANEH S. LATTIMER

Homecoming
Publishing

The author of this book is not a licensed medical professional and does not provide medical advice or prescribe treatment of any kind for physical, psychological, or medical problems. The author only offers information to help you in your journey for greater well-being.

Always consult your physician or healthcare provider before making any changes to your treatment plan.

If you use any of the information in this book for yourself or others, the author and the publisher are not responsible for the outcomes of your actions.

Homecoming Publishing

Potomac, Maryland

www.AltarWithin.com

Library of Congress Cataloging-in-Publication Data applied for.

Cover image & illustrations: Renee Duran
Cover design: Afsaneh S. Lattimer

ISBN: 9780990492726 (trade paperback)
1. Spiritual Wellness. 2. Inner Peace. 3. Self-Empowerment. 4. Spiritual Life.
ISBN: 978-0-9904927-3-3
ISBN: 0990492729
Library of Congress Control Number: 2017919283
Homecoming Publishing, Potomac, MD
First edition, 2017
Printed in the United States of America

For my family and friends whom I've had the great pleasure to learn from and grow with. I would like to thank my grandmother for helping me understand where I truly came from, my parents for setting me on my path in life, and my husband for his constant support and patience – particularly in the development of this book -and for his egoless heart. To my children who bring forth the true meaning of unconditional love and the power of humor. I am indebted to Dr. Robert Rosenthal for his encouragement and support of this book. I am grateful to Hope Connections for Cancer Support, Habitat for Humanity of Montgomery County and Unity of Gaithersburg for providing me the space to expand my love, knowledge, and light. Also to you readers for reaching out for your awakening. And I thank God!

Contents

Preface

*I*f love makes sense to you, then this is the book for you. If love doesn't make sense to you, keep reading.

These experiences reflect my own awakening journey and each of us will have our own unique path. God speaks to, and guides us, in a way that only we can individually understand. So, do not be concerned if your signs, guidance and path are different from mine.

As I learned how to reach Oneness with God, I asked the Divine, "How can I guide my brothers and sisters to remember and trust in You?" In response, God gave me this Guidance:

Tell them that when they feel Love, when they feel that Joy and Beauty in one another and everywhere, that is where I Am.

To experience this Being, imagine a time in your life when you felt immersed in love, in that happy and peaceful feeling. Focus on this, as this is the way you meet him: through your only true emotion, Love.

This was not the only moment He spoke to me. I received much more, not only from God, but also from His messengers. There is nothing mysterious or special about intuitive abilities. We are all able to receive guidance this way. It is simply a matter of being present.

My intention in writing this book is to empower each of us to reach the ultimate state of Truth together, and I hope to achieve this by sharing my journey with You. God is Unconditional Love; and, as an extension of Love, so are You. Now, to clarify six fundamental concepts in this Journey:

What is Love?

Love is expansion and unlimited joy, happiness and weightlessness with no restrictions. It is unlimited possibility and is ever-growing.

What is Ancient Love?

Ancient Love is the forgotten source, God's Eternal Love. Something very old and Infinite. Love that has not been changed and touched with time and space.

What is Unconditional Love?

Unconditional Love means no restrictions and no limitations. Naked to the bone. Doing it, not to look for love, but Being the Love itself. Even time cannot condition It. It is whole and complete.

What is Oneness?

Oneness is You and I and all that is. All that is kind, good and pure. All are equal in the truest state of Oneness.

What is Light?

Light is the constant flow of an eternal power source for all that is and all that will ever be.

What is Creation?

Through our thoughts and beliefs, we are projecting a world that we engage in. Quantum Physics suggests that much of what we perceive in the physical world may, in fact, take its form simply because we choose to observe it. This book is, in part, about choosing a world of clarity.

I was guided to share the messages I received through writing, workshops, talks, and one-on-one spiritual guidance sessions. This book was purposely written to be short, simple, and direct, so that you can sense and experience the teachings. Although it is short, it is not a one-time read, and you are encouraged to read it over and over again. Doing so will help you get connected to your True Self, as well as practice and apply the exercises, tools, and meditations in your daily life.

The information in this book might seem simple, yet it can be challenging to initiate and apply at first. Experimenting with and consistently practicing the tools and meditations will take much effort and self-discipline. Ultimately, they will help you experience an abundance of Clarity to your life's purpose. Your fluid efforts in applying this information will more readily help you align with God's true message. Over many years of workshops, I have had and continue to have a variety of groups, including people with cancer and other illnesses. Participants have experienced greater Inner Peace and empowerment, and have helped others to do the same. When we discover how clarity comes with the knowledge of self, healing for all is inevitable; We are One.

This book does not promote any religion—only love. And the logo on the front cover? That represents how all the answers to the questions you may seek are found through Love itself. The two question marks symbolize how Love is the answer to all and, when you are one with Love, the two question marks meet together to form a heart.

As you study this book and practice the tools with friends and family, you can share and learn from each other's experiences. In addition, you are always welcome to attend our Spiritual Lab (workshops) to receive more guidance.

Be mindful that all change is fearful in the eyes of the ego (the logical mind). If you begin to judge the material, be patient and try to take baby steps. Any judgment will prevent you from reaching Ancient Love. Try to enjoy your life experience, play well together, and have fun! Fun and joy will lead you to a peaceful and loving journey.

—Afie (Afsaneh)

When you doubt your own value, or when you feel less than your full poten-
tial, dive into barriers blocking you from your Light, Joy and Freedom.

Repeat the following, and listen to your Inner Voice:

"I am the driver of my Soul.
I am the Power.
And I am not going to allow a barrier
to stand between Love and Self."
By stating this, you increase your value
for yourself and feel good.
The barriers can no longer block you
from your Light, Joy, and Freedom.
—Afie

One

Rose Garden

God's guidance is so gentle and pure. I believe I have felt His Unconditional Love my entire life. As a child, I felt very close to Him and never felt that He was a stranger. Not by learning about God from books or through a specific religion; but I was brought up with the belief that He is within me, and my connection with Him is true. Most of us believe that we must see and physically feel someone to be close to them, but this simply isn't true. When you love someone, you don't see it but you do feel it. Does feeling but not seeing make it untrue? I often had conversations with Him when I was a child. At the age of twelve, I would sit in the rose garden of my childhood home, surrounded by soft red velvet roses, and I wrote messages to Him on their petals. These small notes were requests for God to direct me in my life decisions, asking for guidance to quiet my mind. It gave me such peace and a pure sense of Oneness. This inspired me to use rose water as a tool for connecting people to their own true beauty and Mother Earth. Rose water represents the mind of God. All water forgives the past and future, clear like the mind of God. Water connects us to the energy of Now.

When I would hear birds in the rose garden, be in nature and enjoy the outdoors, I could feel God's expression in all. The perfume of those flowers, their exquisite beauty, and the songs of the birds were intoxicating. In this tranquil place, I would watch the birds and think to myself, "Oh how free and peaceful they are! They have no need to worry about a thing, and can fly without limits!" Right then, I realized how human beings are more about doing than being. The birds had shown me freedom that we can all become, if only we knew how to choose.

I reflect back on those times in the garden and how I could remember my divine home in the heart of God. My time spent outdoors was a form of meditation, just to be there for the sake of Being. During those quiet moments I would connect to God. Our communion was His way of reminding me who I was—a lesson I would fully learn later on in life. I was always aware on some level that you have to acknowledge who you are in order to connect to God. When away from the garden and with my friends, societal temptation dragged me to the illusion of reality. I could have shared the information I received with them. However I didn't think to do so, assuming everyone had already known. Little did I know, this was not common knowledge. I shared these experiences with my grandmother and, to my surprise, she had already known the power of a Rose Garden.

Two

THE LOVE OF MY GRANDMOTHER

My grandmother was a very influential spirit in my life. As a spiritually awakened person, she would always talk to me about God; how He was someone I could trust and ask for help and guidance. There were so many simple yet profound lessons that she passed on to me. Grandma taught me how to pray, how to quiet my mind, and the way to connect with God. With her spiritual insights, she showed me how to be patient and love others, to not judge and to be who I am. She taught me the meaning of unconditional love. The love that she had for her family and all living beings was so honest and pure. I can't recall a time that she was angry or had judged someone for who they were. She was considered rather eccentric because of her very progressive beliefs and mindset in an era when people tended to hold traditional values. Grandma felt that we, her grandchildren, should enjoy life and show our beauty to the world rather than be modest and hide it.

She was born in 1917 in Iran, at a time when arranged marriages were commonplace. Accordingly, her family prepared her marriage and she later became pregnant with my father at a very young age. She didn't carry hatred for being married so young and missing the opportunity to attend school because she always went with the flow of life. Their marriage was a blissful one and the love and care they shared was immense. She always told us children that our

3

grandfather was such a caring father to their children. He was very educated, and had great handwriting. In his late thirties my grandfather passed away, leaving Grandma with three children to care for on her own. As a female, she didn't have the right to work and support them. Consequently, her family arranged another marriage for her so that she would be taken care of. She then had to marry my step-grandfather, who was a teacher. Together they had two sons but the marriage didn't last long. They didn't divorce, but she separated from him when the kids were older. Grandma didn't see the separation as a negative experience, but accepted the outcome and continued to love her children. If she lacked love or felt deprived of anything, she would rarely show it. More surprisingly, she refused to fear for the future and was seemingly always content. She was the ideal woman to me; strong-minded and carefree.

Even though they were no longer together, my step-grandfather continued to visit my family. When I was in high school, he said I would be a great student for a local spiritual school and that I should be teaching spirituality. However, I didn't attend because I wasn't sure what I wanted at the time. Feeling God's Love was as natural as breathing so it never occurred to me to make others aware of it. I could have never imagined that I would be teaching about God's unconditional Love as I do today!

When grandma visited us, she would stay for weeks at a time. We were connected to her like she was our second mother. It felt so comforting to be with her and it was so soothing when she held us. When we had a headache or any pain, she would put her hands on that place and rub our backs. We could feel the energy coming through her hands. There was something about her hands, something unexplainable—all I knew was that they just felt good. I could feel the love that seemed to heal anything. She had healing hands and she used them because her heart was pure. It can easily be said that Grandma was awakened and totally present, and remarkably she never had a teacher or mentor other than God.

When I was twelve years old, during one of her visits, she woke me up around three o'clock in the morning and asked me to rub her legs. She said she had leg cramps. She always had pain in her legs due to arthritis, so I went to get a tub of warm water to soak her feet in and brought it back to her bed. She put her feet in and I began massaging them.

While I was rubbing her feet, I saw someone appearing out of the corner of my eye sitting on the floor, crouched on the ground, hugging his knees. He smiled at me with gratitude. I didn't say anything but something was telling me that it was Grandpa's spirit. And he was thanking me for the love that I was giving Grandma by taking care of her. I did not want to turn my head or even make a noise because I thought that if I did he would disappear, so I continued to watch him in my peripheral vision. He sat there quietly but I could see and feel the happiness on his loving face. I didn't mention anything to my grandmother, as I was confused about what I was seeing and was more concerned with making her feel better.

I asked, "Grandma, are you feeling better?" and she responded with such a sigh of relief, "That helped so much, my pain has been greatly reduced!" She then told me how much she loved me and how thankful she was for my help. We were both really sleepy by this time and went back to bed.

In the morning when I woke up, I decided to share what I had experienced that night, "By the way Grandma, Grandpa was here last night." She wasn't surprised at all. "Oh, he's always here" she replied. I responded with an astonished look on my face with not much else to say. Hearing this reassured me that what I saw was real, but it still took me by such a surprise. This was the first time I had encountered a Spirit from the other side. Grandma made it sound completely normal to see those who have crossed over. In fact, I now know that she was right. The Spirit never dies and the Love is never destroyed. Her confirmation gave me the confidence to allow my spiritual abilities to unfold rather than shutting them off out of uncertainty.

One time when grandma was teaching me how to pray, I looked at her and said, "Grandma, let's make a promise. If I die first, I will come and visit you. If you die first, you will come visit me." She said okay, "I will come visit you and you do the same." And so we had made a promise. Looking back on it now I ask myself, "how did I understand that we never die and more importantly, how did she know that?" She never said, "Oh, when we die, we die."

When she believed that the Spirit was extremely eternal, it felt good to me so I too believed.

My family would do anything for Grandma, just as she would and did everything for us. She was the love of our lives. She was a chubby, cuddly woman who made us feel safe and secure when we were with her; something very important for a young person when they feel scared and unsure in the world. Grandma was always there for us when we woke up for school and when we returned home.

As I entered high school, I received more messages but I was distracted. I totally ignored the information reaching me. I wasn't really paying attention during this time of my life because I was more concerned with the typical teenage life: sports, friends, clothes, school, homework, etc. While I went to school I kept receiving messages in dreams and wondered what they were. You will find many of those messages as you explore the tools described later in this book.

Three

Reborn in the USA

$\mathcal{A}$fter I finished high school, my parents felt that it was the right decision for me to pursue my higher education in the United States. There were few universities where we lived. To us, the American educational system was ideal. Student life here would be easier with less competition, as there are numerous universities with equally good programs to offer. I didn't question my father's judgment and fully accepted my parent's guidance. This made it less difficult for me to leave them and move abroad. Also, I knew that in order to fulfill my life purpose I had to come to the US and complete my education. At the time though, I knew very little English. My knowledge of it consisted of the alphabet, numbers, and some basic vocabulary. I couldn't understand nor speak the language. When I applied for a student visa during the 1970s it wasn't as difficult as it is now to obtain one. I applied to study English at an American university before starting my degree and was accepted.

I was so very excited to be going on this journey to a new place with so many opportunities. I felt so hopeful in that I had a purpose to fulfill here. Immediately, I immersed myself in the unfamiliar culture by living, studying, and socializing, and after one year of the English language training, I was ready to begin my college coursework.

Within the first year of living in my new country, I had a significant encounter with God's Spirit. I dreamt that I was in a house full of people whom I didn't know. All was well when suddenly there came a flash of brilliant yellow and orange Lights. The entire house was consumed with this massive orb of energy. I was awestruck with its beauty and could not resist its powerful warmth. But as I turned my gaze from it, I noticed everyone else possessed fear in their eyes. Some yelled, "Let's hide! Let's hide!" So they hid in the cabinets and under the beds—any place they could find to take shelter. I was left standing there by myself. I thought, "Why are these people afraid of this amazing Light? I'm going to open the front door and invite it in. It feels so good and has done no harm, why not embrace what it has to offer."

As I opened the door, I saw a beautiful, massive sun float down to the entryway. The warm glow was so comforting that it filled me up with overpowering Love. The sun smiled at me with gratitude for opening the door. All it wanted was to share its overflowing light so I happily smiled back without any fear or complaint. I stood still in shock with the feeling of Joy. This Love and Light was so familiar to me that I couldn't understand why these people were afraid of it. The heat was so comforting and loving that since the morning I woke from the dream, I have never forgotten the experience. The feeling was all too real and pure. Over time I have pondered as to why the others were so afraid of the sun, and still couldn't understand why. Later in my life I had realized the purpose of the dream in my sleep: These people were so fearful because they were afraid of Love. I awoke feeling incredibly hopeful and knew that I had a purpose to fulfill.

Shortly after that experience, though, I was occupied with balancing full-time employment and school. I was very distracted with making ends meet but I wasn't upset because I was enjoying my life. I was enjoying the freedom of doing things for myself because back home, other people were always doing things for me. It felt good to be independent. I learned many beautiful lessons from life, including how to not be needy for love, how to dust yourself off and move ahead, how to be fearless, and that feeling lonely is poisonous. Throughout all of my lessons though, I never forgot to call on God for guidance and support. Messages came to me but I rebelliously ignored them and acted like a child, thinking that I could handle everything by myself. Figuratively, I stopped writing messages on the rose petals, but I still heard a voice that told me that I had to ask for help to pull me out of my fearful thoughts. In my fear and confusion, I wanted to continue playing in the illusion. So I chose to experience life without fully understanding the consequences of ignoring my gut feelings, which were actually telling me that these toys and situations would hurt me.

Quickly though I acclimated to my new life and always stayed in touch with my grandma through letters and phone calls while she was thousands of miles away. When I was in my early 30s, I was able to see my grandma back home one final time before she crossed over. A few days after her passing, she came to me in a lucid dream with her guardian Angel. I can even see the Angel so clearly now. She was dressed in a translucent, white, weightless, lace gown, and her wings were also made of the same glowing material.

This divine being gently pushed the door open and came into my bedroom. I could see the Angel leading my grandma by the hand as they floated to the side of my bed and stopped and looked down at me. I knew as soon as I saw them that they were here to say goodbye to me in the physical form. I was so happy to see my grandma because she fulfilled her promise to visit me after her passing. Grandma gently moved her right hand to touch my arm but the Angel knew that Grandma was not aware that we could not physically hold each other anymore. The Angel told her through in the language of spirit, which I could understand:

You can not touch her anymore. She knows that you are here to say goodbye to her in the physical life. You can still connect with her, although it will not be through physical touch.

The lucid dream was so vivid that I wasn't sure it was actually a dream at that time. The next day, my father called and I told him, "Dad, I had a dream about Grandma." Every time I said this, the phone line would disconnect. I called back and said, "Dad, I saw Grandma. She came to say goodbye." The phone disconnected again. This wasn't happening due to a bad phone connection, but rather her way of letting me know and acknowledging that she really had come to visit me and she wasn't gone. Leaving her body behind was simply like changing her clothes to go on to the next level.

Meanwhile, I was pursuing my degree in Health Science Education and one of the required courses for the program was an anatomy class. On the first day of anatomy lab I saw a cadaver lying on a table and thought to myself, "It can't be. This body is a piece of nothingness lying here. How could this body have had life before?" I later learned that this man was a former professor at the university and had donated his body to the science lab, but I could clearly see that there was no value in that body. I knew that our Spirit was indestructible and always connected to God; however, this was my first realization that perhaps the physical wasn't what it appeared to be and that without our Spirit the body is nothing. Still I had to learn all the parts of the body in order to understand the marriage between mind, body, spirit and emotions.

Quickly I became busy with life again and got married, while also studying, and soon thereafter earned my degree. I entered the field of health education and was working with abused children and teens, their parents, and battered women who were experiencing serious issues and unimaginable trauma. In helping them process their emotions about these painful events, I realized how people often focus on the past and make decisions for the future only to lose the present moment. And that when a person makes decisions, while focusing on their past experiences and hurts, they choose suffering and are not able to make decisions that would serve their highest good. Even though I was helping others during that time period, I was disconnected from the present moment. In those days, it took me the better part of an hour to drive between my home and work, and I often didn't even know how I got home from the office in the evening because I fixated on those children's problems and sadness and wanted to help them so much. But their problems made me realize that I could focus on the solutions.

Ultimately, my work during that time period gave me a great deal of experience in talking before people and counseling. It was a connection to people that prepared me for the work that I'm currently doing.

Nevertheless, I was overly stressed from my work responsibilities - to the point that, when I was pregnant with my first child, I began to experience early contractions in my second trimester. My doctor ordered me to come see him at the hospital immediately - at which point he told me that I needed to go on bed-rest for three months until the baby was delivered; otherwise I would lose her. Without hesitation, I permanently left my job and stayed home with my daughter after the birth to take care of her. Despite the nine month pregnancy, this still felt like a sudden and profound transition. My new life in America, my efforts to educate disadvantaged children, and the all-consuming responsibilities of motherhood would both shape and validate many of the lessons that I teach in my workshops – and that we will explore in detail throughout this book.

Four

The Tunnel and Light

Five years after the birth of our first child, we relocated to Maryland. We eventually settled in a home where we would raise our children. As soon as we moved into our new house, I could feel the presence of the previous owner's deceased husband, a man of only fifty-some years in age. He played a major role, through his spiritual presence, in helping us purchase the house. We were a young and eager family ready for growth and a place to call our own. Something that he had always wished for his own family. He had made much of an impact on us and, in his honor, I placed electric candles in each window of the house that are always kept on. So he helped us settle into our home rather comfortably, despite such a painful struggle it was to move from Florida to Maryland.

Before settling in our new residence, I first had to face one of the most challenging episodes of my life. I had to adjust to so many changes. Not only did I miss what I considered to be my home and life in Florida, but also I was six months pregnant with my second child. And living in a new area meant that I needed to find a local doctor whom I trusted, which was a very difficult decision for me. Someone I knew had recommended a skilled physician who had retired, although still ran his own practice, so I went to meet the doctors working in his office to choose my new obstetrician/gynecologist.

The first time I went to this office, I felt uneasy and anxious. I knew something wasn't right. I rationalized it by telling myself that I moved here from a small town and I'm in a big city now. Doctors' offices here are probably always busy, that no one has time to interact with their patients, and the buildings are older and small. But I didn't listen to my gut feeling that I should have immediately left and chosen a different practice because I had a good feeling about all of the OB/GYNs except one with whom I felt uneasy. Once again, I was distracted at the time and ignored my intuition.

My previous doctor in Florida and I agreed to have a cesarean birth since I underwent the procedure with my first child. The surgery was scheduled for the Monday after the Thanksgiving holiday weekend. As it happened, I went into labor two days before the surgery date, while my new doctor was out of town. As I experienced bleeding and contractions, I was admitted to the hospital as an emergency patient. The only doctor on duty happened to be the one whom I earlier had mixed feelings about. During my initial check-in, I asked the nurse if there was another doctor who could perform the delivery because I knew that I did not want this doctor to operate on me. I had an overwhelming feeling. The nurse told me that my only two options were this OB/GYN or an intern since the rest of the medical staff was on leave for the holiday. It didn't make me very happy, but I had little choice other than to work with the doctor.

Before we went into the operating room, the doctor tried to persuade me to have a natural birth. Yet, I knew that a C-section was absolutely imperative, based on consultations with my own doctor, and so I refused. She agreed to go ahead with the surgery and while I was being prepared beforehand, I noticed that there was someone standing in the room watching and listening as the doctor talked with the anesthesiologist. I asked the doctor who this person was and she responded, "Oh, she is an intern. She is here to observe and learn." That was fine with me but I explained that I did not want her to be involved in performing the surgery. The doctor didn't respond. In fact, she completely disregarded what I had just said, as I saw the intern pick up a scalpel and begin to make an incision on my lower right abdomen.

The surgery, which had been completed in under half an hour for our first child, dragged on for several harrowing hours. Though I had hoped to remain awake to welcome our new child into this world, I would eventually need to be completely anesthetized. As I went under, I found myself in a long, pitch-dark tunnel. I was very confused and afraid, as I began sliding faster and faster through it over bumps and was flung wildly from side to side at a dizzying speed. It felt like riding a dark water slide—I did not know where I was going or what was happening and I began to scream. It was gloomy, cold, hopeless, and lifeless in this winding tunnel. The turns and curves within it became less erratic, as the tunnel began to straighten out. Suddenly, I could see a bright, promising Light at the end guiding me, while I felt my speed slowing down. It was warm, comforting, and reassuring. Immediately, I knew there was nothing to worry about and I was being taken care of because this seemed like the radiant Light that I had encountered in my dream after I arrived in the U.S. and my feelings in the garden.

When I was approaching the Light, I heard a Voice say that I had a choice to either remain on the other side or return to my physical life and everything is going to be fine. In hearing the Voice, it reminded me that it was not time for me to go Home yet. We are programmed so that when we see the Light, we remember where we came from and who we truly are.

I knew that I was not ready to go yet—I still had things to do. I had to take care of my babies. I was not done yet. Once God's Light came fully into view, I felt His Love and wanted to go back and expand It. I craved to let people know that Divine Love and Light are always here to serve and nurture us. It was so clear to me that my story was not finished, as I instantly remembered why I was here in this life. I remembered my purpose. So I told the Divine that I was choosing to go back to the physical world and play more. Since I was determined to return, I wanted to Be and Do just as the Light inspired me to have trust and Faith in God, which meant fearlessly spreading the Love, Peace, Light, Beauty, and Comfort that I experienced here from then on. Most importantly, I needed to share the truth I had found with people. Who they truly are, their identities as children of God. Because of my decision, I did not reach the end of the tunnel.

When I awoke, I saw myself being rolled down the hallway from the operating room back to my room. My whole family was anxiously waiting there for me, wondering why the procedure was taking so long. As I came into the room, I saw the look of shock and worry on their faces. I learned from my husband that the surgery about four hours. Everything went wrong this time. My husband said that, as the surgery dragged on over those hours, I appeared ever closer to death - my face graying, my eyes beginning to roll back. He would eventually leave the operating room and plead with the staff to summon another doctor. Eventually, another physician arrived. In time, the assembled team were able to complete the procedure but not before I had lost an extensive amount of blood – and gained a life-altering insight.

It was very fortunate that I was so insistent on having the C-section because of the placenta Provera complication that I wasn't even aware of since my local doctor had neglected to share this with me. However, the operating room doctor would have learned this in my medical files if she had read them. Without the procedure, a natural birth would have killed both the baby and me. I later learned from the hospital staff that this physician had little experience and was uncomfortable with performing a C-section delivery so she wanted to avoid the surgery. Nonetheless, my resistance created a fearful environment for myself, and I was going against the flow rather than just being. What I didn't know though was that I had to go through this experience to meet God again and that I would be all right. This was just the beginning of my journey, although it was actually my second wakeup call to remind me who I am. I knew that I had to experience this Light once more and spread it.

My recovery was a slow, year-long process as I was very sick and weak. Quickly I had forgotten about my experience of crossing over while recuperating and taking care of my newborn son. However, a few months after the surgery, I began to remember the messages that I had received. This experience led me back to my Ancient Home (I will explain in further detail in the next chapter what our True Home is) and returned the memory of who I am and why I am here. Because of it, I knew that I had been chosen to fulfill a purpose in this world, although I wasn't exactly sure what I would be doing. However, I was aware that I needed to connect to God like I did as a child, to find out what He wanted me to do in this world. Soon though, I forgot about this experience and my life purpose as I spent a year recovering from my difficult C-section and focusing on taking care of my family.

Only now, years later, have I realized that my ego had tried to block me from reaching my Truth. I was speeding and sliding past my sad and difficult experiences in life. The fear and guilt disappeared because I wanted to pass through it and that's when I saw the Light and decided to choose it over the darkness. By being fearful and lost, we swim in our madness and choose darkness in the forms of sadness, anger, stress, depression, anxiety, or victimhood. It wasn't time for me to go Home yet as I needed to go back and expand this Light and let people know that God's Love is here for them.

Five

A PROMISE KEPT

After my "near death experience," my awakening journey began to unfold very quickly. In 2001, my mediumship abilities rapidly began to unfold. Whenever I talked to my dad or spent time with my family, I would hear my grandma speaking as if she was sitting right there with us. She would even come and give me short messages about our family members, which of course, made me start to think I was going mad. So to test if she was really visiting me, late at night after everyone else had gone to sleep I placed a doll on top of a very high cabinet that no one else could reach, and thought to myself, "Either you are here, Grandma, or I'm imagining things. If this doll is on the ground tomorrow, then you are here. If not, then I'm imagining things." The next morning, I had totally forgotten about my test and went downstairs to straighten up the living room. There were children's toys strewn about and when I saw the doll I wondered what it was doing on the floor. It took me a moment to realize the significance of its placement, but once I knew what had happened, I wasn't surprised at all to find it there. I was so happy to know that my grandma was still with me.

She came to me again as I was talking to one of my children about something they had done. While I was speaking, she appeared and in a loving voice said to me, "Don't make a big deal out of it. Everything is fine." I responded to her, "Grandma, now is not the time." As soon as I said it, I was shocked to find myself speaking out loud to her as if she were physically there with me. Ultimately, her many messages and visits fulfilled her promise to visit me if she passed first and to tell me about the other side. She wanted me to know that there is no such thing as death and we are eternal beings loved by God. More personally, her message expressed, "LOVE NEVER DIES!" as our love for each other continues up to this day. After this message I trusted her guidance and her presence, and fully understood that death is an illusion.

Six

Seeds of Miracles

---

*D*uring the Christmas of 2001 while I was out of town, my mother was taking care of my dog and the house and thought it was sad that my Christmas tree was unlit during the holidays. She decided to turn on the Christmas tree lights since the house was dark and just before she did so, the lights turned on by themselves along with music. My mom called me screaming in shock and crying, "Afie, you won't believe what happened! The Christmas tree turned on by itself and was singing!" I thought there must be a logical explanation for this. "Maybe it was plugged in," I told her. She insisted that it wasn't. The frantic tone in her voice along with my awareness that there were spirits all around us convinced me that the lights had turned on by themselves. When I returned home after the holidays, my whole family gathered together and prayed in the room where the Christmas tree stood.

At this time though, I knew something was happening. My grandmother taught me to stop and pay attention to signs, such as when I saw my deceased grandfather's Spirit, because there was something I needed to hear. And since I had had a few extraordinary experiences, like with the sunlight dream and crossing over, I knew that something was happening. I had a feeling that there was something I needed to know and perhaps the incident with the Christmas tree lights and music was a message of some sort. Being that

Christmas celebrates Jesus' birth, I wondered if perhaps he had something to do with my tree lights and music. Since I had been receiving messages from my grandmother and her guides, as she tried to always steer me to the light and Spirits, I thought maybe I could also receive messages from other entities, like my guide Nure. My sense was that both Nure and God wanted me to know they would be with me and help me during my life transition. I had never studied the Bible but I believed in Jesus being a prophet, and more importantly, this message felt good. It was very comforting because I always felt that I'm here for the purpose of bringing peace to people even though I didn't know how I was meant to do this yet.

Changes kept happening. In 2002, I discovered a late night spiritual program on public television that featured a speaker by the name of Eli Jaxon-Bear. He was teaching about the Spirit's freedom, the illusory nature of life, and how to attain inner peace. Some concepts, like the illusion, didn't make sense to me at the time but what he was teaching felt good, and I couldn't wait to watch his program each week at midnight. The reason I was so excited wasn't clear but the information seemed oddly familiar—it felt comfortable. Like before, the information lingered in the back of my mind but I had so many other priorities that seemed important to focus on at the time.

Seven

HEALING MIRACLES

*Y*ears passed as I continued raising my family and going through the daily routines of life. However, my awakening journey intensified in 2008. That year, a family friend experienced a life-ending heart attack just before her baby's due date. It was a shocking event but paramedics were able to take her to the hospital where the baby survived 45 minutes without oxygen while waiting to reach the emergency room. His delivery was successful but that time without oxygen left the newborn seriously ill and so he stayed in the intensive care unit of the hospital for treatment.

Something had told me that I had to go there and see him. So I went with my family and met his father at the ICU. As I was looking at the baby in his small bed, I received the message to place my hand on him even though he was attached to several machines that took care of his every bodily need. Standing there, I felt a gentle nudge on my back from my guides to place my hand on his arm. As I did this, my guides then physically led me by the arm to pick him up and hold him. Following the guidance, I asked his father if I could hold him to which he surprisingly answered that the baby loved to be held. Carefully, the father unhooked the tubes that he could and handed him to me for a short holding since he couldn't be disconnected from the machines for too long. He was so relaxed and comfortable lying in my arms. While resting there, the newborn gave me the message of happiness and that life is good. This infant came here to play with enjoyment even though he was completely paralyzed to the extent that he couldn't even swallow on his own. Some of us may think that this was no life at all and that death would be preferable. However, with this experience, my guides wanted me to remember what life is all about. They wanted me to see his pure love and be aware that we were not separate. When I held this boy I did not even notice the wires, just his unconditional love. His Spirit was telling me, "No matter what situation I am in, I still love to create and I am grateful for just being here to play with Joy!" At the same time, I wasn't sure why my guides wanted me to use my hands on him until I later attended my first Reiki class.

Not only were my guides introducing me to energy healing but also the concept of the ego. I watched an interview on Oprah Winfrey's television show with an author by the name of Eckhart Tolle. The two were discussing his latest book, A New Earth. Everything that he covered during their conversation made perfect sense to me about the ego. Not only did it feel as though I had read this book and The Power of Now before but the material was so familiar to me that it felt like I had written it. When I found out that Oprah was also hosting on her website a weekly study guide for the book, I quickly went out and bought it and began the self-study program. Going through the program helped me to remember why I was here in my subconscious mind— to spread God's unconditional Love and eternal light. It felt awesome reading the book and I finished it so quickly.

After finishing Tolle's books, I told God that I was ready to get to work and had been asking Him, "What else do you want me to do?" Within me, I knew that my guides were making plans but I was unsure what they were. I heard the message from God that I needed to get a pen and paper to write down the information that I was receiving. My mind was so busy and this was one way to remember everything that was coming to me. Plus, I had already been doing this as a child. I also heard that I needed to read more and that I must meditate to quiet my mind. So I picked up more books to continue learning but my meditation practice had stalled. The first time I meditated was in 1979 in a Mind, Body, Spirit college course. Although I had stopped once the class finished, I resumed a regular routine in 2006. Each time I meditated, my hands would tingle, which I assumed had something to do with why my guides urged me to hold the disabled newborn. It also reminded me of my grandmother's healing hands; perhaps I could do the same with mine, but I wouldn't understand this fully until studying Reiki later that year.

Eight

A GUIDE FOR GOD

A few months thereafter, I was given another experience of being with God. I love mornings. There is something about the energy in the morning that is very powerful. Most mornings I like to exercise by going for a walk around my neighborhood, but I began to have some unusual experiences at a particular point along my route in late Summer of 2008. One morning, I left the house and turned onto Lochinver Lane, which is a short street that winds up an incline and then straightens out as it slopes down past a small brick school behind my home. I've always felt that there is something indescribably special about this path. As I started walking down the slope on one walk, I experienced an overwhelming feeling of pure Love. It was so strong that I wanted to sprinkle this Love and Joy on everyone. It was as though I was returning to a familiar place - somewhere you always felt comfortable and happy.

On another walk, I took the same path. I turned onto Lochinver and following the curves then the downhill slope of the sidewalk and passing the school, I inexplicably felt the urge to spread out my arms and close my eyes, as I flew down the hill. Giving into my impulse, I could see myself on top the world, looking down upon it from outside of my body. I then knew that I came here to be a guide for God, to introduce and expand His unconditional

Love for us all. In spreading this Divine Love, He wanted me to lead people out of confusion and help them come to know who they Truly are, where they came from, and what this life is all about.

It felt phenomenal to be on top of the world with God's guidance and to be One with everything. I was so charged and happy, It was like I was flying so free as the birds from my childhood and completely weightless. Love comes in varied colors, like a rainbow, and surprising ways such as when someone smiles at you or holds the door for you. I felt Love expand, becoming more beautiful and brilliant, like a blooming Rose. The whole scene evoked the image of the powerful "Christ the Redeemer" statue overlooking the city of Rio de Janeiro. Shortly thereafter, the figure appeared in my local newspaper. Upon seeing the picture of Jesus, I connected it to my walk, and I then heard the message that I was shown the image as a sign to trust that I was being trained to be a guide for God.

Two weeks after that experience on top of the world, I awoke early and sensed a message from the Holy Spirit—the connection between God and us—that I needed to go outside for a walk. After taking my son to school, I set out on my route along Lochinver and soon came upon a feather lying on the edge of the sidewalk at the bottom of the hill. The color of it was positively striking—I had never seen such a feather before. As soon as I laid eyes on it, all judgment ceased and I left the illusory world. That feather started talking to me. It reminded me of who I Am and why I came here, similar to the times that I experienced the light in my dream and in the tunnel. I began to remember the purity of my Spirit. This feather brought me the gentle touch of God upon my shoulders, infusing me with His Happiness, Laughter, Joy, Freedom from worry, Release, and Peace. It brought me right back to the rose garden, where I spent time with Him as a child. In finding this feather, I received the answers to all of my questions. My find opened up my spiritual sight to the present moment and I saw the truth about myself in this journey. It was like looking through an ethereal lens to see the true world of Divine Love and Oneness And while I was taking in this new world, the feather gave me the message that "the Sonship is coming." I didn't know what "the Sonship" referred to or its meaning, but it was clear that we needed to love one another, not judge ourselves or others, become aware of our Perfection, and know that we are One with God. At this time, I knew that my life was just beginning and that brought me even more Hope and Joy.

The following day, while I was walking and looking down at the sidewalk, out of nowhere I saw a pair of legs walking beside me. I noticed a man's toes curling to grip his brown-strapped sandals, as he walked along. I looked up to see there was a tall, graceful man dressed in a long, tan robe next to me. I was not surprised at all when I saw him because he felt very familiar. He was quiet and just continued to walk along with me and I sensed that he was my main guide. Every so often I would notice him, for instance when I meditated or performed Reiki, so I asked him his name. The message came that his name was Zakarya. He had been with me since I was born and would stay with me until I crossed over. We all have a guide, who remains with us throughout our entire journey in the physical world. Zakarya's purpose is to protect and support me, and bring me peace. And since he's always with me, even when I'm not aware of him, I can call upon Zakarya any time I would like for absolutely anything.

Our guides also serve as a conduit to the Source, since you can't get there by yourself. They will lead you, so once you get to know them you're all set and would never feel alone again. But you first have to be in a state of love and gratitude in order to trust the guidance from your guide and then you can reach the Source.

With all of these extraordinary experiences that I had along Lochinver Lane each morning, this short road symbolized the place where I remembered the Truth. It was here where I discovered my altar to the Divine. The very top of that street felt so good and the feather was my present from God, waiting for me at the end of it. I knew that if I trusted the guidance that I was receiving then I would succeed in fulfilling my promise in this journey to spread His Love to everyone, even if I didn't know exactly how I would do this. I attempted to listen as I quieted my mind, at which point I received more guidance as I tried on the lenses to my new world. Things became clearer and clearer and are still becoming clearer to this day. Ultimately, the sight of this feather woke me up in Heaven, and gave me the message that I need to spread God's tenderness and teach about His devotion for us. It was the key to unlock my awareness of who I was and have always been as an expression of His unconditional Love. With this knowledge, it put me on the right path to reach my True Home again and experience the ever-present protection that our guides provide for us in our journey through life.

On so many occasions I had received messages from the Divine but I kept diving back into the dream again and succumbing to societal pressures to fit in. Out of nowhere this extraordinary feather appeared and I just saw the beauty and love in it because I didn't judge it or analyze its appearance. The message came through non-judgment; otherwise, if the ego had taken over, I would not have received the message.

At this point I was curious about the feather's symbolism, and while I was looking at the trees I received a message from the Holy Spirit about "Togetherness." The branches on each tree looked like hands so I researched it online and came across Dr. Doreen Virtue's work. She said the feather is a sign that angels are all around you and they are trying to get your attention. I had had a sense of this already but I wanted to make sure my hunch was right. I also felt that the angels were showing me God's Love and reassuring me that I was on the right track. Yet, my next step wasn't clear so I attempted to connect with them and asked, "What do you want me to do?" The answer didn't come right away, but rather the next time I went out for a walk. I came upon a pair of trees whose branches extended to each other as if each was reaching out and holding the hand of the tree next to it. They locked limbs so tightly that they merged into one enormous tree, casting a massive shadow to show me the idea of Togetherness and <u>One</u>ness. I found myself extending my hand to join them. This single tree symbolized how important Fellowship is for our peace and freedom and that the Sonship is coming. Soon I would understand that the Sonship represents humanity's love for each other, freedom, and eternal unity that is true <u>One</u>ness.

Nine

The Gift of Revelation at the Beach

---

*L*ittle did I know that the feather experience was preparing me for a third encounter with God four days later. For some unknown reason I had an urge to go to the ocean and meditate at sunrise, although I had never done this before. I thought it was a great idea and with the Labor Day weekend approaching it was the perfect time to go; but I couldn't take credit for the plan, as I would later learn. The Holy Spirit and my guides actually gave me the message that I needed to go as though it was my own idea and urge, and it seemed like they were taking care of the arrangements to ensure that I went on this trip. Rehoboth Beach in Delaware was only a few hours away, so I looked to find a place where my family and I could stay. Being a holiday weekend, everything was virtually booked in the popular tourist town but luckily we were able to find a small guesthouse one block from the beach.

Our first morning at Rehoboth Beach, I woke up around 5:15 and walked down to the water in the dark, as the sun began to color the sky. Right when I reached the sand, the warm, glowing Light of the sun appeared on the horizon. It was beautiful and so unlike anything I had ever seen before that once I saw it, I fell to my knees in tears. When the sun touched the edge of the ocean, the whole world stood perfectly still. Everything stopped, including time and space. The illusory world of duality disappeared, even my physical body, as I merged into the reality of pure Unconditional Love. All judgment ceased and I was One with God. With faith and trust I placed myself in the hands of the Divine, as I flowed into the Heart of God. My <u>Oneness</u> with Him was all that existed.

The full awareness of our <u>Oneness</u> was so powerful and overwhelming that I could not stand on my feet nor feel my body. The Power of God's Love was so immense and stunning that tears of joy streamed down my cheeks once more. I was overcome by a sense of Wholeness and Completion that made all of my concerns and needs totally meaningless. They completely evaporated with my tears. I cannot fully describe it. I went to my True Home, to True Love, to True Freedom. It was everything. It was a miracle. And during this experience, God revealed His presence to me. Words are not strong enough to express His passion for us!

As the world stood still, it was like everything was melting away and I did not want this euphoric feeling to go, but it gradually drifted off. Then God gently, although seemingly at the speed of light, brought me back into the physical life, telling me I could not stay in this intoxicating state of Wholeness because I had work to do. Uncontrollably, I wept tears of gratitude, as I thanked Him for His gift. It took me some time to recover from the shock of this experience and unimaginable Beauty.

I knew afterwards that my life had changed for good; I felt immense Hope and great Joy the rest of my journey. I became someone else with this Attunement from God, as His Love washed over me. Somehow I understood after this powerful experience with Him that I was Spirit, which is constantly connected to the Source, and not the body. The Attunement led me to re-member my Higher Self; it felt so good to be connected to my True Self and the Source. And I knew that I was reborn and did not want to go back to my old self. Not only had my perception of myself changed, but I also was aware that this is not the only world and definitely not the real world.

As I walked back to the guesthouse where I was staying, the houses that I saw did not look the same to me as when I had first walked down the beach before dawn. Nothing that I saw felt real to me anymore and I knew that none of it was. It was an illusion. The real world is pure, Unconditional Love and I really wanted to go back Home but I had a lot of work to do in the meantime.

Everyone was still asleep when I returned to the guesthouse so I decided to make myself some tea. There was no teakettle in the kitchen but I was able to use a pot to boil the water. Once the water was steaming, I took the pot from the stove and began to pour the hot water out of the side into my mug. Without a spout to guide the scalding water, I accidentally spilled all over my left hand. I looked down to see how badly the water burned my skin. Surprisingly, there was no pain at all—not even redness or blistering. And eerily my hand appeared as though it was someone else's, like it was my old hand. In that moment, I felt as though God was telling me that He was with me as I re-experienced that Love from the beach. My mind was free of all thoughts and worries, and I started talking to my hand and told it that I am not choosing pain, not now. I desperately wanted to stay and meditate more at the beach. However, this attunement from God validated for me that I was Spirit and not my body, which empowered me to see my True Self and stay calm so that I didn't choose to experience any pain. I had absolutely no doubts about my decision. This works for all of us. If you really want something, then nothing can change your mind.

In hindsight, I believe the hot water incident was a message from the Divine that I needed to go forward with my decision to help others and that I am being taken care of at all times. Actually, I knew since my childhood experiences with my grandma that we are being nurtured and spoiled by the Divine at all times. But after avoiding the hot water burn, I knew for certain that God constantly protects us and that nothing could ever hurt us. This invulnerability came from my awareness after I met God and joined with Him at the beach that I am totally complete with my Source. And since He is everything and I am one with Him then I am everything and have everything. What more could I possibly need or want?

Ten

"WHAT ABOUT INNER PEACE?"

J was looking for a way to share with others what I had experienced at the beach and learned from my guides. In the course of reading, I learned that when you want something, write it down and ask your guides to bring it to you, in alignment with the law of the universe. I prayed and asked my guides to teach me God's Light, Peace, and Love through tools to spread and share with everyone. In total faith, I knew that if I asked for what I really desired, not requesting out of lack or neediness, then I would receive my wish. I prayed extensively to receive tools and guidance, and the message came from my guides:

> *You are not done yet. There is one more step.*
> *You need to work on your inner peace.*

I thought They meant that I had to become more peaceful, more relaxed. Then I asked my guides, "What about inner peace?" They responded:

> *You need to read the inner peace book.*

So I went online and searched for an inner peace book but I couldn't find anything by that title. Since my web browsing efforts turned up nothing, I doubted the message and believed it was just my imagination. Yet, if I had trusted the information as I do now I would have searched more thoroughly.

Nevertheless, I began reading as much as I could about spirituality and forgot about the "inner peace" message that I had channeled until I studied Reiki II. As I was reading through these books, feeling on top of the world and filled with total joy, I wanted to know what other knowledge and tools I needed to help people reach that stillness and Joy I was feeling. So while I was out on a walk, I asked God for guidance. Again the message came that I wasn't ready yet but I needed to be patient and continue reading more books. My guides added they would protect me and take care of me on this journey. As I later learned, they are part of a group that is here to lead us Home, and they reassured me that they were by my side. They repeated this over and over again, although I couldn't shake my doubts that I was making all of this up.

Healing with Him

Over the next six months, I was receiving several messages and was totally confused about what they meant and what exactly my guides wanted me to be doing. Every time I meditated, my hands still tingled and became boiling hot. I knew that had something to do with my hand not burning following my encounter with God at the beach. At the same time, I received messages that I had to use my hands to do energy healing—either Reiki or Qi Gong—so I looked both up online. Qi Gong didn't excite me much. But in my research on Reiki, I located a teacher in my area and called him to find out about his classes and class dates, although I wasn't really sure what Reiki was.

The teacher initially asked me why I wanted to study Reiki. He felt that I didn't need any training in the healing modality. All I needed to do at this time was just use my hands. I said to him, "No, you don't understand. I have no idea what's going on." He was very relaxed and patient with me as I had so many questions about my spiritual path and heightened intuitive abilities. After our conversation, I couldn't wait to study Reiki with him.

When I attended the first day of class during the Autumn of 2008, I knew that it was exactly where I was supposed to be. The heat in my hands during my meditations and my guides' instruction to hold the helpless infant was guidance to expand God's Love and peace through the practice of Reiki. And I found that the practice of Reiki quieted my mind, enough for me to be able to clearly hear the messages that I had been receiving from the Divine and those who had crossed over. In turn, the doors opened up and helped me fulfill a part of my life that I needed to realize.

A Course in Miracles

After completing my Reiki II training, I invited some of the other students to my home for a Reiki share. During a break, they were discussing their favorite spiritual books. I happened to join the conversation as one of my classmates was talking about *The Disappearance of the Universe*, written by Gary R. Renard, whose book provides an introduction to the principles of *A Course in Miracles*. Several mentioned that the Course is published by the Foundation for Inner Peace. That grabbed my attention because my guides had told me to find a book on inner peace. So I asked if such a book really existed and they responded "Yes!" My search was over. This confirmed for me that the Course was the book my guides were instructing me to study all along. When they told me about it, all I could hear was "*Inner Peace.*"

After receiving so many messages about what I needed to do, such as studying *A Course in Miracles*, the pieces of the puzzle were coming together. I needed to work on my Inner Peace! As soon as I found out there was a book about this, I knew God had a big plan for me. My life was about to bloom and things became clearer as answers to my questions emerged.

Later that evening while I was giving Reiki to a client, her cousin who had recently crossed over came and gave me messages unlike anything I had heard before. He was only in his mid-twenties when he passed but there was such maturity, wisdom, and a sense of playfulness in his words. He wanted his family and us to know that we are all visitors here on this planet for just a short time - so we should appreciate life because it is so brief. We should enjoy every moment of it instead of being worried. Life is just a movie—it is child's play, a game. And all of the items we possess are just toys that shouldn't be taken so seriously.

My client was shocked to hear this. She then asked me if I had read anything from the Course before because the concepts of life as play and the toys of the earth are covered in the book. I had never heard these ideas much less heard of the Course before that day. It was rather strange timing though that right after I learned of the book, such a unique message would come from her cousin. He provided subtle confirmation that this was the book that I had been looking for. I went right to the bookstore, bought *A Course in Miracles* and immediately began my studies. After absorbing its many lessons, I paused to reflect upon them before moving on to read Gary R. Renard's *Disappearance of the Universe* and *Your Immortal Reality*, both of which instantaneously made complete sense to me and complemented Eli Jaxon-Bear and Tolle's work about the ego. On my spiritual journey, I needed a reminder of who I was and what I came here for, and these books were a wakeup call to get to work and complete my mission in an exhilarating way.

Once I started reading *A Course in Miracles*, the book totally changed my life. The document was channeled by Helen Schucman from Jesus in which he shared the way to reach Love and peace through the forgiveness of our illusions, which we will discuss further in the next chapter. The self-study curriculum is composed of three sections, the first of which is the Text that outlines a thought system with the purpose of learning about Love and forgiveness. The second section, the Workbook, allows you to apply and practice the Course's teachings through 365 daily lessons. And the third section consists of the Manual for Teachers and an explanation of Course terms.

In the writing process, Helen took down in shorthand notes Jesus's information and then dictated the material to her colleague William Thetford who transcribed the entire document over a seven-year period. Thereafter, Kenneth Wapnick, Judith Skutch Whitson, and Bob Skutch assisted in organizing, publishing, and disseminating the book through the Foundation for Inner Peace, and the organization continues to spread and teach its message today.

When I began to read the Course, I felt at home. I knew immediately why my guides wanted me to read this book and it was clear that I was exactly on the right path. It was a second chance to complete my mission in this lifetime, and find the clues to the puzzle that I had been looking for. Even now I am still piecing the clues together with the help of Jesus and those involved with the book's creation. I am so grateful for my experiences that made this book possible. In reading it, the information it contains showed me exactly how to fulfill my life purpose.

As I began to read the Course, Jesus became my Spirit Guide and teacher. All this time he had been slowly over the years introducing himself and subtly preparing me to become his student. I first felt that he was trying to get in touch with me when my Christmas tree lights and music mysteriously turned on a few years earlier. He had probably given me other messages, too, but because of my distractedness I had likely dismissed them. He never gave up on me and, through his gentle efforts, he was easing me into the Course and its material. It felt so right and that this is what I needed to know all along. During this spiritual education, I was renewed with the feeling of completion, which was so exciting that nothing could stop me from growing and expanding.

In the western world, Jesus represents an enlightened prophet who is working to help all awaken, and every religion has their own prophets. Regardless of your spiritual background and beliefs, a prophet of the same Spirit will guide you to Divine Love as well if you wish. There are many ways to God and that is why we have many different spiritual books, hold different beliefs, receive different messages, and experience revelation in different ways from my own journey. I believe that the Course is the fastest way to reach inner peace.

In my personal experience with my teacher, Jesus led me step by step through each chapter of the Text and instructed me when to read it and when to stop. If I kept reading after Jesus told me to put the book down, the material would make no sense to me. Yet, the message of the Text was so familiar that I knew I had already studied it in perhaps other lifetimes with him.

To complement the Text, Jesus even provided me with examples and lessons in my daily life of what I was reading in the Course and taught me the meaning of my personal lessons. Essentially, he was preparing me to see the illusory nature of life, which we'll talk about in great detail in upcoming chapters. Once I finished the Text, Jesus instructed me not to start the daily lessons in the workbook yet. I did not start lessons because I did not feel ready, yet the message was so clear. I would find out six months later why he was so insistent that I wait.

Eleven

RAISING SPIRITS

While studying the Course, I was conducting Reiki sessions with clients. As I was working with individuals, the message came from Jesus, "Don't focus on the body. The pain that people have is not physical but you are paying attention to the physical." So I said, "Okay, what should I do?" He told me that I first need to talk to the individuals because the problems that each of them experiences are not physical, they are emotional - in the unforgiven mind. The stress that they are feeling is created by their thoughts and their bodies are responding to these negative thoughts by becoming ill. I had a sense of the importance of our thoughts during my Reiki training, particularly during the second level class as I began receiving messages about the causes of people's illnesses. Since Reiki focuses on the body and the body is an illusion (as I learned with my grandmother) I instead used Jesus's method of healing by seeing individuals as He did - in a loving, non-judgmental way. Jesus saw the purity of God in everyone - the true innocence of their Spirit (TRUE HEALING).

My teacher was totally right as I witnessed my clients' results. By talking to people, I can discern if they are fearful, stressed, depressed, or confused as well as see the root cause of their fear and guilt. Based on the severity of what they are facing, I can gauge how much guidance each person needs and then, using my intuition and with the help of my teachers and that of the individual, I design a personalized GPS system (based on the tools listed in subsequent chapters) to lead them back to the right path.

Once people bring their fears, anxieties, and stresses to the surface by talking about them, they can then release those feelings during the healing session. People don't realize that they're confused because of the past and guilt they may be carrying for things they did or did not do. They also may be concerned about the unknown course of future events. Once they see where their fear, guilt, and self-punishment come from, they can view them in a different light and start to forgive both themselves and their past or future fears. At this point, they can release their fear and guilt to reach a place of peace where they are receptive to the loving guidance and energy from the Divine. Essentially, the entire healing session is a detoxification process, as they let go of the fear and guilt that block their awareness of the Divine's ever-present Love. In turn, they become comfortable with themselves and are prepared to receive God's gifts and guidance. If they are ready to receive these gifts, then I can guide their Spirits and walk with them to the Land of Heaven, the Land of Peace that is the foundation of inner peace.

In the beginning, I wasn't sure. I thought maybe I was just imagining this information from my teachers. Often we don't trust the messages and we judge them, but this doubt blocks the guidance we are receiving. This is an issue for all of us.

As I continued to study the *Course*, I received more messages confirming that the approach of first talking to the individual would facilitate their healing - but there was another step I needed to add to the process. One day I just happened to be looking out my living room window when I was surprised to see Jesus's face reflected in my neighbor's window across the street. He said to me:

You need to do this work. But with healing, first you have to send people my messages, then you can give them your teaching. You must talk to individuals to guide them to the Light of Heaven and help them to see who they are and why they are here. Tell them about their life lessons, forgiveness, how to love themselves, and try to build their foundation and then the healing will affect them.

Not only did I need to first talk with people, but now I also had to share the messages that I was beginning to receive for them. Soon thereafter, clients' guides along with my own came to deliver messages. When I did this during healing sessions, the effect was very powerful. Many people left feeling like a changed person as they felt a deep peace that they had never experienced. Their Spirits traveled to places they'd never been to before. The peace and calm they felt was so good that they had a difficult time coming back and opening their eyes, and they didn't want to come off the healing table.

Teachers and Guides

Within six months of completing my Reiki II training, the healing energy changed to Qi Gong and then Divine Light Energy, as I worked with people. One afternoon I was performing energy healing on a client and I saw an Angel on my right side. She was short in stature and very serious but also very caring and loving. I asked her, "Who are you?" She told me she was the Angel of Divine Light Energy and to relax so that she could help me perform my healing work. Her job was to send energy through me to the client and she also instructed me in performing certain techniques to balance the client's Spirit. The Divine Light Angel's gentle guidance for the client and myself was like someone hugging you and telling you, "Do not worry."

A month after the Divine Light Angel appeared, more helpers joined Zakarya and Jesus, including Mohammed, Nure, Joseph, Razmaraj, Mehr, Mother Mary, Abraham, Nicolas and Einstein. These teachers and guides belong to the "Group of the Fatherhood", which is here to help shepherd us all Home. The leader of this Group is Jesus who was always with me.

Zakarya founded the Group of the Fatherhood. He's the gopher and organizer. He came with the feather and then started looking for what I needed. He is also the branch manager of the Group of the Fatherhood and has the power from God to bring each Soul what they need. He selected the members.

He had asked for my help to heal people's minds, and guide them to discover who they Truly are to reach total peace. One evening, I was online checking my email when unexpectedly I had the urge to meditate. This happened to be another instance of my guides giving me subtle guidance without my knowledge. I didn't go right away but later that night I went into my living room to quiet my mind for 15 minutes. Jesus immediately appeared, kneeling down at my feet and looking at me with immense Love in his eyes. Right away I was struck by his peaceful and soothing presence. I didn't want him sitting down on the floor, though, while I was comfortably resting in a chair. Knowing what I was thinking, he then said to me, "Don't feel bad. You are worthy of my Love and praise." As he said this, a feeling of Joy and a powerful sense of merging with God came over me. But I was also astonished by Jesus's humility—his words carried neither arrogance nor an air of superiority. All I could see was his purity and loving heart as he emanated peace and Joy.

While he kneeled there, down on the floor, I wanted to nurture and mother him as though he were my own son. For some reason I've had this motherly feeling towards him since I began reading the Course, although this feeling isn't unique with just Jesus. I've always had an impulse to nurture everyone since I was a young girl. Jesus then went on to say, "Mother, I need your help." I was stunned to hear him call me this just as I had been feeling like he was my own child. He also viewed me as a mother figure, which made me wonder if I had been his parent in another lifetime.

My teacher became quiet but continued giving me messages with his loving gaze. Through his incredibly beautiful and comforting eyes, he shared with me that he needed me to spread his Love and peace in this world. This encompassed the work of a guide for God, a role I was specifically chosen for. I told Jesus that I would do anything in my power to help him, of course with his guidance. I could sense that he already knew I wouldn't refuse his request or react fearfully, especially since he and his Group of the Fatherhood had been testing my readiness all these years.

I was so happy and excited to be picked for the job that I wanted to give Jesus a big hug. I felt that I was getting closer to what I always wanted to do in bringing peace to others. So with my eyes still closed, I opened my arms to embrace him. He raised himself up on his knees and hugged me back then slowly he faded away. Instinctively I rubbed my hands together and brushed them over my face, as I returned from what felt like an exquisite trip to a beautiful place.

I was beyond excited to take on the job but I felt that there was so much that I needed to learn in order to be a knowledgeable guide. The most important thing I needed to know was the Truth so I asked to be shown this and taught its meaning. At my request, Jesus' other teachers, Mohamad, Mehr, the Divine Light Angel Nure, and Joseph began to prepare me for my role, almost as though I had a contract to fulfill, but one that I couldn't wait to undertake. Accordingly, every day they guided me in how to heal and how to bring more love and peace to people, and they gave me tools to help forgive others and ourselves.

Twelve

GIFTS AND TOOLS FROM ANGELS– THE COTTON BALL

*T*he healing was working for people, yet in late 2009 I asked my teachers and guides for additional ways to help others. One afternoon as I was working with a client, the Angel of Divine Light appeared and wanted me to share with this person a message about a cotton ball. Not seeing how a common household item could help my client handle challenging situations in his life, I thought the cotton ball was ridiculous. But after the Angel of Divine Light explained to me the simple message behind the cotton ball, which was meant to be used as a tool to help this individual, I was convinced to use it. After I finished the energy healing session, I told the client to take the following steps:

1. *Get a cotton ball and fluff it up as much as you can then hold it in the palm of your hand. Do not be afraid. Just fluff it. Do it without any hesitation.*

2. *Now close your eyes or sit quietly for a minute and go within. As you feel the cotton ball, feel it with your heart. How does the cotton ball feel? What does it look like? Take a moment to study it and get connected to your inner Voice.*

3. *Sit quietly and experience the pulsation of your thoughts.*

What you are feeling right now is your Spirit. Your Spirit feels so unrestricted, free, gentle, and weightless. There are no complications and no struggle to fix anything.

Are you nurturing yourself (thinking delicate thoughts of gentleness, non-judgment, and certainty of perfection) just like this cotton ball? It is like a newborn baby (pure and innocent) and symbolizes how the Divine sees you.

4. *Now take the fluffy cotton ball and twist it as hard as you can until you squeeze out all the air and make a knot out of it.*
5. *Hold it tightly between your thumb and index finger.*
6. *Sit quietly and ask yourself how the cotton ball feels as a twisted knot.*
7. *Take your time to experience the pulsation of your thoughts and feelings.*

The knot you have just made represents your pain body and confusion that will attack your body parts. In nurturing the knot rather than answering its wakeup call, the knot manifests as physical and mental illness, ranging from a headache, to a common cold, to clinical depression, to HIV/AIDS, to cancer. The knot also symbolizes:

1) *a block to seeing the Truth in the Light of the Divine;*
2) *the fear of the unknown and neediness for Love;*
3) *our pretending to be God-like and mis-creating; and*
4) *closing all the doors to the forgotten power of You and the Divine.*

But by being present and building your awareness of your thoughts, emotions you discover how to undo the knot.

knot=confusion+pain+suffering
+judgment+shame+blame

The fluffed cotton ball represents our Spirit that is Love, Joy, Peace, and Freedom. Conversely, twisting the cotton ball symbolizes when you judge yourself and invite fear into your space. The good news is that you can always bounce back from the knot (pain, suffering, and judgment) to the fluffy cotton ball (our eternal Spirit). This means rejecting the fear and returning to Love. Undoing the knot will provide you with ways to release your pain and suffering that are created by the thoughts in your mind (infused with belief in the imagination) to escort them out and to create joy (the imagination is used to unlock and open the doors to possibilities, without judgment). You can carry this cotton ball with you throughout the day as a reminder that you are a free and unlimited Spirit.

Thirteen

"Be Loud and Clear Like a Rooster"

The simplicity and brevity of the messages and tools from my teachers always astonished me. They wanted my teaching and guidance to be simple. Life is simple however we don't see it as simple. It is all about love. One of the first things Jesus told me was, "We picked you to be simple." It makes sense to me now looking back on the simplicity of all my notes (channeled messages) from that first year. Nevertheless, I wished to be more expressive in conveying messages to people as English is not my first language but Jesus kept repeating to me to be simple in my teaching. In fact, I received the message that they purposely chose me to do this work because, as a non-native speaker, I have a tendency to express things in a simple and straightforward manner. This way I would be less likely to complicate the messages. And in sharing their guidance, my teachers told me "be loud and clear like a rooster," meaning don't be afraid. Be proud to share this information without any doubts. The rooster also symbolizes an awakening, bringing people from darkness to the light. In this new beginning of my life, I was prepared to follow their advice as I had made a promise to God that I would do anything He asked of me to spread His Unconditional Love and Light.

The information kept slowly coming, one step at a time. The following year, I was invited to a party. I wasn't really in the mood to go out that night but Jesus firmly told me that I needed to go because "the people there need your light. You just need to be with them." He was insistent that I had to go and connect them with who they are; to help them start loving themselves. As I had done so many times before, I questioned if I was really hearing this. Immediately, Jesus responded that I was not dreaming what I had heard and so then I knew that I wasn't going crazy. Literally, though, he commanded me to go to the party and kicked me out the door. I was glad I went because I was able to share his guidance with individuals there who were experiencing confusion in their lives.

Similarly, over Christmas that year, Jesus instructed me to speak at a church where my family attended services. Again, I had no idea what he wanted me to talk about before a highly educated, upper-class congregation. But Jesus was very firm, saying:

> *The world has not changed since I left over 2,000 years ago. The toys may have changed and people may seem more educated now. Yet, no matter how much money or education they have, they are still lost souls, meaning they are still searching for true love, joy, peace, and happiness.*

I thought the minister would already know about <u>One</u>ness and Forgiveness so who was I to tell his congregation about this? Ultimately, I didn't speak at the church because I didn't have permission to do so, but Jesus assured me that more opportunities would come to speak in front of groups. And he was right. More opportunities did present themselves to share my messages along with those of Jesus, the Holy Spirit, and my teachers.

"Be bold like a rooster!"

Fourteen

TOGETHERNESS AND THE LAND OF LOVE

That same year I was asked if I would meet with a group of senior citizens to talk about my spiritual work, which I was reluctant to do because I wasn't sure what to say. Nevertheless, Jesus encouraged me to go and work with the group as older individuals often have so much fear and lack Love because of their feelings of hopelessness and helplessness. One's light is so dim in that state. Moreover, they all needed to forgive their past. As it turned out, the group wanted to hear the messages that I was channeling about love, peace, suffering, anger, forgiveness, kindness, tolerance, and Togetherness. That one meeting turned into weekly meetings with the group over a number of months and that's how I began holding workshops—it was a process that didn't just happen overnight. Initially, though, I thought that I was writing down insignificant bits of information rather than channeling since the messages were so short. However, I would hear someone repeat them on television or in a conversation, or read something similar in a book – and that confirmed that the messages were meaningful. Once I began to trust them, doors began to open up and the information became more detailed and lengthy.

While I was channeling in a notebook information for the group, I again received messages about "Togetherness." The Holy Spirit wanted me to share with the seniors that:

Together we can build a stronger relationship, a stronger bond, and heal one another. We all need one another in order to reach Heaven, and once we are together we will be in total peace. We are not separate. We are <u>One</u> in the Heart of God!

I was shown the meaning of this message and how important it is to reach <u>One</u>ness through Togetherness in one of my meditations some time later. As soon as I closed my eyes to meditate, my teacher Mehr appeared and gestured for me to follow him. We walked through a long, very crisp, bright white corridor until we reached a door at the end of it. He opened this door to reveal behind it a green land with trees. I thought to myself, "Why is there open land at the end of the corridor?"

Quickly I forgot my question as I surveyed this place. I noticed that the land was kind of quiet, like it was longing for something. Mehr then lovingly told me, "This is THE LAND OF LOVE." When Mehr said this, as if waiting for their cue, people dressed in long, cream-colored robes gracefully and gently came out from behind a forest of powerful, sagacious oak trees and formed a line before me. These enlightened beings all looked alike, although I could not make out their faces. They were very quiet but one being stepped forward from the group and said to me:

We have been waiting here patiently for a long time for Love and Peace. We need your help and we need you to guide people Home to Love and Forgiveness. We want <u>Oneness</u>. We cannot be complete until we are all <u>One</u> with God. We can meet each other through peace and Love for one another—not through fear and madness. Judgment should stop because people are judging, hating, and killing each other. We are waiting for you to help us. Please teach others about Love and Forgiveness so that we can return to our eternal Home. Love is what brings closure to all of us, and we will wait as long as it takes.

It was clear that they had been waiting for a very long time for us to come together with Love. I responded, "I would do anything to bring Love, Peace, and Forgiveness to the world so that we can all go Home Together." At the same time, I was struck by their unwavering faith that in the end we will make the decision to love and care for one another. They wanted us to be in peace and trust that God is taking care of every<u>one</u>. From this encounter I learned the meaning of true <u>One</u>ness. These enlightened beings, who have finished learning their life lessons in the physical form, are patiently waiting for all of us to love one another. They know the Sonship is coming.

Fifteen

Signs and Dreams – Unrattle the Ethical

In the winter of 2009 I awoke around four o'clock in the morning to the sound of Angels and enlightened beings from the Land of Peace marching to beautiful, soothing music and drums. The music was quite loud but I couldn't see where it was coming from. I thought it might be from people outside on the street but there was no one out there. Unable to find the source of the sound, I went and washed my face to wake myself up since I must have still been dreaming.

In my confusion, I went back to bed and drifted to sleep while the music slowly faded away as though the Angels and beings were marching further down the street and eventually out of my neighborhood. However, they had wanted me to hear it to get my attention and so the Band of Divine beings departed once they knew I had heard the joyful sounds. When I awoke in the morning, the music sounded very distant but I could still hear it. I wished to hear it again at full volume yet it stayed with me faintly throughout the day.

I didn't understand this at that time, but it seemed like the Angels and Beings were marching and playing music to celebrate my awakening from the illusion of life—it was the music of Heaven. With this experience, I started to believe that this life was not the only one we could experience. There is music that we can hear if we quiet our mind, and there is true life somewhere beyond here.

My dreams became much more intense and I was receiving more guidance. Once I dreamt of being in a classroom all night with the Holy Spirit, learning about spirituality. At about three o'clock that morning, I was wakened by a loud, male voice speaking right next to my ear. It was so loud that I knew I had to write down his message. I heard, "UNRATTLE THE ETHICAL!" I had no idea what it meant and fell back to sleep.

When I woke up later that morning, I sensed that I had been listening to a lecture all night although I couldn't remember anything that I had learned. Suddenly, I recalled that I had written something down on a piece of paper. I checked it and it said "Unrattle the ethical." I asked myself what the phrase meant. Jesus told me, "Don't look for people because they may not be ready to receive your messages. We will send them to you." Immediately, I knew he meant that I should not challenge someone's beliefs unless they are ready to receive the Truth. Moreover, if they're not ready to receive healing, let them be. The message made perfect sense to me and up to this day I've been following Jesus' and the Holy Spirit's instruction to let people come to me for guidance and healing.

As I was receiving all of this information, I knew it was all true but my ego was fighting me about the messages and my life purpose. One morning, I headed out for my morning walk and I was talking to God. I demanded to be shown something totally unexpected, not feathers or coins, which I always came across. I wanted something so out of the ordinary that it would prove to me that all of the information I received was valid and not a figment of my imagination. I wanted concrete proof because the temptation of my ego and my doubts were slowing me down in my journey.

While I was walking along my route, I heard a voice direct me to turn right onto a street that was not part of my usual walk. The voice directed me to the high school in my neighborhood where my family had watched a football game six weeks earlier. While watching the game, my husband dropped the stylus for his cell phone in the bleachers. We all had checked the field and stands several times and there was no trace of it. Yet on this, sensing I was being led to the high school, I wondered if they planned for me to find that stylus.

As I predicted, once I reached the school grounds the voice guided me in the direction of the bleachers. Approaching closer to the stands, the Holy Spirit, Zakarya, and Jesus told me to slow down. As I slowed my pace, they instructed me to look down on the ground. Just a few inches from my feet was what looked like an eyeliner pencil. Still I had doubts that it could be the stylus and said to myself it must be a makeup pencil. I picked it up and tried to write on my hand with the object but no ink came out. Looking more closely, it was indeed the lost stylus! I was so shocked and excited that I called my husband and told him the news.

It may seem like such an insignificant find. Yet I was so happy knowing I was in God's hands that I felt like I had just won the lottery. From that moment on I was sure that He had been taking care of me since I was a young girl. And I was incredibly grateful that He sent Jesus, the Holy Spirit, and my teachers and guides whom I trusted to heal and lead me every step of the way in my journey.

As a healer and guide for God though, I still had a lot of work to do. First, I needed to heal myself before I could effectively work with Jesus to heal others and this could only be done by balancing my ego, disciplining my mind and thoughts, and learning how to love and forgive.

Sixteen

The Comfort of Your Mind is the Home of Heaven

With all of this information pouring down, I still had endless questions and a relentless desire to find the answers. I continued seeing clients through my healing work, which provided so many extraordinary experiences, while I was reading the Course with Jesus. I also went to a variety of workshops and attended a weekly Course study group to learn as much as I could and I asked Jesus to walk with me every step of the way. And at my request, he was always with me. Every time I would read the Course, I asked him to guide me in understanding the book's concepts, although it felt like I had studied this material before in many lifetimes.

Everything bloomed when I studied the Course. This book answered my questions about what I needed to do in this life. I first had to attain inner peace and then I could expand that peace to others, as the Course teaches. However, I didn't want to just understand these ideas by reading the book. I also wanted to experience them and the peace the book described and I also asked Jesus to show me every detail of how he learned and experienced true Oneness with God. But Jesus didn't want me to start the daily lessons just yet, as I mentioned before, for reasons I would later learn. So he and the Holy Spirit used my daily life experiences as a classroom to provide me with lessons and training in order to be a guide for others. I knew this was all I wanted to do and that it was my passion in life. To be successful in my new job, I asked for help in disciplining my mind and the temptation of my ego, and to bring me tools and guidance to spread light and God's Unconditional Love to the whole world. In response to my request I then received guidance from Jesus, God and others. I was very surprised that I was connected and getting messages. I couldn't believe that my teacher was here and guiding me. The journey was becoming so exciting and I couldn't wait for my lessons. Every day was a gift that I happily unwrapped as I prayed to be shown the Truth and only the Truth.

One morning in the winter of 2010, I woke up and asked to know what my daily lesson was. The lesson came in the form of seeing my son sick with a severe allergic reaction. We didn't know what caused the rash and as we tried to figure it out, I asked God what my lesson was in seeing this and what did I need to forgive - I had forgotten that the body and physical pain are controlled by our minds and not actually real. Only our thoughts make the body and pain appear real. So by perceiving my son as a body that was ill, I was making the situation very real for myself and then I became fearful.

The answer didn't come immediately, but the doctor eventually determined that the rash was food and cat-related and so he prescribed a medication to alleviate the symptoms. I drove straight to the pharmacy, which was very busy with customers and employees rushing around on this workday afternoon. After picking up the prescription from the pharmacist counter, I headed to the checkout line where there were eight people in front of me. I noticed that there was only one cashier working the registers and so the line was moving pretty slowly. In the background there was a cacophony of noise between the store music playing, the phone ringing, and people complaining there needed to be more cashiers to help out. The whole scene was pretty frantic.

While standing there, I asked Jesus again why I was seeing sickness through my son. I remembered that we were not made of sickness, pain, or suffering and there is none in God's Heart; so what was my lesson? Suddenly, I experienced being taken out of my body by the Holy Spirit and brought to this place of total peace and stillness. From this tranquil place, I observed the whole scene from a removed perspective. The music and noise faded. The people moved in slow motion. The cashier and customers looked like mindless programmed robots without any awareness. Behind me, all of the store shelves were stocked with little, empty pillboxes, just like when a child plays doctor. Nothing appeared real to me; everything looked like props on a movie set. I then turned to my right to see where my son was. He was standing there beside me, like a robot. I reached out to touch the top of his head and make sure that he was there but I saw him as another character in my play, like my little toy doll that was pretending to be ill while he was playing.

Even as I saw all these people as mindless robots, acting out their as-signed roles, I still felt great love for everyone and enjoyed watching the scene without any worry or judgment. All of my previous anxiety and concern for my son had totally disappeared as I looked on this trouble-free world. My attention then shifted from my son to a woman who finished paying the cashier and walked past me towards the store doors like a programmed robot muttering, "I can't believe there is only one cashier." Very slowly, I turned my head to look at her and heard the Holy Spirit tell me, "There is no place to go. Why are you angry and rushing?" Seeing that the woman was really just a robot, pretending to be upset and short on time, I watched her leave the store and disappear.

Just as I looked back at the cashier, everything suddenly fast-forwarded and the music and noise returned, creating the frenzied, loud scene I had witnessed a moment earlier as though nothing had happened. I was in total shock. I didn't know what had just transpired but I then knew that there is no one else out there. There is only one Spirit and the world we experience is merely the projection of thoughts in our mind. These projections include all of the people we see and interact with; we project each individual and object with our thoughts.

In asking God for the lesson behind my son's sickness and why I was see-ing sickness, the Holy Spirit had shown me something quite mind-blowing and totally unexpected. The Divine revealed that I had created the situation for myself since there was nobody else out there in the world. In forgetting that both the body and sickness are just our thoughts projected outward into the world, my ego brought me fear and worry.

With gratitude I saw the power of the mind and the power of the ego as I progressed in my journey. I trusted Jesus and the Holy Spirit to bring me my lesson about the ego with this experience, which was the best classroom that the Holy Spirit could have used to teach me what is really happening in the illusory world. From this look behind the scenes, I learned how much power we give to the ego in our mind and how our mind projects our thoughts like a movie projector. It also exposed how unreal this life of illusion is and how easy it could be to forgive people once we see the reality of our thoughts' projections, knowing that we created the robots we see and therefore they cannot harm us. How simple it is to turn around negative life experiences to see the goodness and the lessons in them. It also showed me that I could be in this illusion but still be connected to the Source; in other words, be in this world but not of it. This was the start of my journey and the information came and showered me with goodness, pure Love, and total peace. That is when I said I am ready to expand God's Unconditional Love.

Divine Lessons

As I shared my pharmacy experience and the accompanying messages with a fellow group of students, the event didn't make sense to my audience. I asked them what the meaning was behind the experience and what I needed to learn from it. They were anxious to hear my story but didn't seem interested in relating my experience to any of the lessons in the book. We instead went on to read the book rather than talk about all of our life experiences. It seemed as though they couldn't see the value in my lesson and weren't very interested in practicing the Course's teachings in their everyday lives, which really surprised me.

After the study group experience, I realized that I needed to ask my teacher Jesus, why people were so confused and what my lesson was from this event. As Jesus told me:

Be one with the information and one with God. Finishing the Course is not the goal. It's about understanding, living, and being it. You become one with the book and like meditation, merge into the power of the Divine. If you do not, you just go through the same endless maze thinking you're spiritually advanced but you are still feeling separate from one another and one with judgment.

Jesus' message made perfect sense. The group's reaction helped me to see how confused people in the world are, even those who are reading the Course and how they didn't understand the Text's message and didn't really live it. Rather than understanding the power of the mind, these individuals were giving power to the physical world, their body, and things that didn't feel good like pain, guilt, and fear. Feeling guilt or fear or physical pain supports the ego and empowers it to guide us to the darkness where we ignore the present moment. It is in the present moment where we find the power of God. So any time we are in the past or future and not the now, we lose our connection to God as well as our own power. However, we also are no longer connected to the Source of Unconditional Love and Oneness, which is who we are (WHO WE ARE). This is the ego's whole goal; to keep us separate from each other and our Source so that we cannot remember our true authentic self, and the individuals in my Course group unknowingly fell into this trap of feeling separation.

In addition, I learned from my Course group that some people do not understand that this life is a dream and also a classroom to teach us how to love and forgive one another. But before the dream began, there was and has ever been Heaven, our ancient Home. It is the perfect Love, peace, Oneness, wholeness, and completion that we came from but have since forgotten. However, I'm not saying "Home" as in where we go after we die and cross over to the other side because that place is neither eternal nor where our Spirit came from. The other side is part of the dream of life and death where you look at your report card and see how well you did in learning your life lessons during your many incarnations. Each of us must take the test of choosing how to love, forgive, and be kind to one another in the classroom of life until we successfully pass the exam. This classroom is really a tool to bring us closer to God in which we experience duality and contrasts like happy and sad experiences, fear and Love, guilt and peace, light and dark. In reality, there is no such thing as duality because there is nothing but pure Love. Love has no opposite. Duality is another example of a sharp toy that separates us from Love. In reality, there is nothing broken and everything is in perfect order so whatever we're experiencing in life is what we need to learn. Don't struggle with the lessons because then you won't learn it and see the miracle. It's easier to pass our lessons with the help of the Divine in making our life choices rather than trying to control everything ourselves and play God.

Once you review how well you did in learning your lessons in each illusory life, you can then choose to re-take the test if you're not satisfied with your grade and reincarnate again to learn your forgiveness lessons. Or you can stay on the other side and learn these same lessons in that illusory place. Nevertheless, some make the choice to be lost on the other side in their confused state and have chosen suffering if they're still angry at how they crossed over. Perhaps they were killed in an accident or by another person and assuming weren't ready to leave at that time. They came to send messages to each other and instead of delivering the message of choosing forgiveness and accomplishing what they were supposed to learn they become confused.

However, the majority of individuals want the human experience so that they can come play in a physical body but then forget that they have to take the test of choosing how to Love, forgive, and be kind to one another once again. In this case, they forget who they are, why they came back, and they stop studying for their exam by not choosing Love and forgiveness. That's fine though because it's part of the journey that we choose for ourselves. Yet, if an individual passes all their lessons and learned how to forgive themselves and others, it would set their Spirit free to reach to eternal peace (HEAVEN), which is part of who we are because we are an expression of God's love and His beauty. Saying it is easy but doing it takes lifetimes, and you must be mindful to always invite God into your space for guidance, which makes it easier to reach the freedom of our Spirit that is <u>One</u>ness.

Seventeen

FORGIVING SELF

For my next lesson, my teachers wanted me to understand there is no order of difficulty in miracles. So they presented me with another classroom experience, using the idea of illness, to teach me that there is no degree of intensity in pain and suffering. All illnesses, whether it be a headache or a terminal disease like a cancer, are all the same. Their cause is the result of our projection of fearful and guilt-based thoughts. Some of you may think right now, "I didn't choose suffering or purposely create a negative situation for myself." Yet, this often happens unconsciously. Those who cross over with various illnesses came to this life purposely to bring us a message to help us in our journey, and when they cross over, they never feel any pain or suffer as we see and feel it.

If we are experiencing any kind of illness, the good news is that we can turn around any uncomfortable and painful situation regardless of how severe it may seem and feel by disciplining our fearful thoughts. The tools and exercises that my teachers had been providing me proved that there was no order of difficulty in healing all illnesses generated by our thoughts.

For instance, I had a neighbor who learned he had stage four cancer in the fall of 2009. Through his wife He found out that I performed healing work so he asked if I would give him a healing session. During the first session, he experienced a peaceful garden with beautiful flowers that he couldn't describe but they were a beautiful, bright yellow color and brought him a great sense of peace he never felt before. Afterwards, he repeatedly asked his wife if I could give him healing every day. I tried to give him healing as often as I could for the short while they lived in the US. He became so relaxed during sessions, and then one day while he was receiving treatment at the hospital, his wife called me. She said he was asking for me to visit him there. I went over to the hospital and talked to him for a while and gave him guidance, but the message that he gave to me was so powerful. After performing a Reiki session, he opened his eyes halfway said, "I have a message from God. He is telling me that 'I am sending my Love through Afie's hands to you. Please, receive the Love. Be open to receive. And the only thing I want from you is to love yourself, stop beating yourself, and love others.'" When he told me this, I said, "You need to love and nurture yourself and stop torturing your physical with your fearful thoughts." He shook his head in agreement but was afraid of changing his direction.

The last time that I saw him was at his home. I told him, "You're giving up, aren't you?" I could see in his eyes that he didn't let the fear go. I asked him if the fear he was feeling was bringing him any peace. He became quiet and looked at me. He started crying and didn't want to talk about it. I said, "You know you can turn this around. The pain that you're feeling is not physical. You can turn around the cancer. You can get healed if you make up your mind. It's a choice." But he had so much fear and guilt that he said, "Afie, I cannot let go." He already made up his mind. There is a reason he was here—for other things but to also bring me the message. So I took that message and I used it to heal myself and other people: The first step of healing is to be fearless in choosing Love. And from my dream in which I was told to "Unrattle the ethical," I had to respect his choice but I didn't need to uphold it.

My teachers were presenting me with different life experiences to show how powerful fear can be and how quickly it can destroy us when we give power to fear and the past. This message was a gift from my teachers to assist me in my life journey to see and feel power only in Love.

After his passing, he came to visit me in Spirit with a very powerful message. He had discovered that what I was saying was true as his lack of fear on the other side helped him to see the Truth. He told me, "I filled up my physical with crap. I filled it up with junk. I filled it up with madness. I filled it up with anger and fear." He had a good sense of humor but the point of his message was that people can choose to treasure their body by filling it up with Love and compassion. Choosing to fill up your body with beautiful things is the way to reach <u>Oneness</u>.

The lesson that I learned was so beautiful: we can fill up this mind with beautiful things rather than garbage, fear, stress, judgment, and anger. When you fill up with negative things that don't feel good, you're only hurting yourself. Thankfully we still have the opportunity to change our thoughts about an illness even after we cross over, although we're no longer in a body, but we can still experience the light of Oneness and pure Love. We are then temporarily healed in our mind but when we come back to this life we may forget the lessons we learned from past lives for a little while or we may remember them right away. It is our choice to accept Love or fear. Some people may get a little better but still they need to work on their forgiveness lessons while others may choose to stay on the other side and study longer. Those who are angry and fearful tend to want to come back right away and start the insanity all over again but more likely at a later age or in their next lifetime they will choose to let go of their fear and accept Love.

Eighteen

Show Me the Ego and Its Tricks

One day I found myself with a rare break in my usually busy schedule and I thought I would enjoy it by going out for some fun shopping and relaxation. As I was driving to the store, I was thinking to myself how good it felt to relax when my cell phone rang. I answered the phone and it turned out the caller wanted to know if I could do them a favor. People often call me, asking for help with small issues and sometimes with very serious ones, and I always try to lend a hand but on this particular day I really needed some time for myself.

On this day, my caller asked if I could pick up something for them at the grocery store right away. They told me it was okay if I couldn't do it but I instantaneously felt like I couldn't say no to this person. This can be particularly challenging with family members, which is an example of the ego's special relationship that can hurt and emotionally drain us in our journey. Feeling obligated to help out, I decided to postpone my shopping trip and go to the grocery store even though I had only a little free time.

Angrily I hung up the phone while I was waiting at a red light. I started talking to myself and debated what I should do when I heard a voice tell me to turn right, which would take me onto my relaxing shopping trip that I was really looking forward to. But since I was in a bad mood, I turned left instead. As soon as I did, I heard a calm and loving Voice instruct me, *"Pull over and stop. Think first. Quiet your mind and think clearly. What would you like to do?"*

My teacher wanted me to consider my decision but I ignored the guidance because I wanted to stay annoyed and miserable. By doing this, I was only hurting myself because the other person had no idea that I was upset and they didn't mean me any harm with their request. Still I chose anger instead of putting myself first and being true to my own needs and wishes to take a break. As a result, I was making a series of decisions that led me to judge myself and the situation and become very upset.

In irritation, I continued to drive. Once I reached the parking lot of the grocery store, it was so busy that I had to look for a parking spot. Finding a space between two vehicles, I pulled in but miscalculated the size of the electric truck in the next spot and grazed its protruding bumper. The noise of scraping metal was like a jolt that woke me up from this angry dream and released all of my aggravation.

Disappointed, I asked the Voice, "What is going on? You are supposed to help me." The Voice replied, "We tried to but you weren't listening." I then laughed and asked myself, "Why didn't I listen?" The voice of the ego and its rage was so loud, yet it felt so good and promising at the time, that it drowned out the loving guidance I had received. I took a deep breath and thought to myself that the addiction to feeling miserable and righteous anger is very strong and a sneaky trick of the ego, or the wrong-minded thought system that we engage when we choose pain and suffering. After learning my lesson, I felt so calm that I forgot all about my anger and even the damage to my car. I was overtaken by a feeling of joy and gratitude the rest of the day, knowing that I was being protected and guided at all times!

That night, I returned to my classroom by meditating to see what I needed to discuss about the incident with my teachers in a state of stillness. They responded that my lesson allowed me to taste the poison of the ego without hurting myself and experience how it traps you without your awareness. I saw that when you are aware of your connection to pure Love, the ego's poison does not affect your body, mind, Spirit, or others. In other words, when you don't give power to things in your mind, like fear or guilt, it has no power over you. I also realized I needed to nurture and be truthful to myself, as well as all living creatures.

Nineteen

THE ROAD TO TRUTH

As I was searching ways to share the experience of who we are, I kept hearing the message that I am a guide. In order to guide people to God and feel his Unconditional Love, I felt like I needed to know where we came from otherwise I wouldn't be effective in my role. I would think "Where did we come from and why are we here?" One day, while talking about Jesus and his healing messages, information came to me that I knew I needed to write down. I picked up a pen and started drawing. I had no idea what I was sketching but it was like someone else was controlling my hand. On a piece of paper, I drew a circle, and then I could feel God's presence in the room. Next I heard Jesus say, "*This is where we came from. We are like a seed.*" Speaking for God, Jesus meant that this seed symbolized the moment in which we seemingly left our Source. This separation began as God's Son was just wondering what it would be like to leave his Home in Heaven and pretend to play like God by himself. He was curious for a split second. "What if there were things besides Love, peace, and Oneness? What would happen?" The Son was playing with Love and wondered what would happen if he stopped loving. His curiosity created these questions (and we all know that curiosity killed the cat) and the Son's imagination fueled these insane thoughts. While asking these questions, he forgot to smile at such an outlandish idea and, in that moment, the Son took the idea seriously and panicked. In that instant, the idea produced a little spark of a thought that flew away and fractured into countless smaller sparks that created a seeming sense of separation from his Source. The Son continued imagining what it would be like to be separate and, as he was thinking, he fell asleep right next to God.

As the Son was napping, he began to dream and in his sleeping state he created both the mind and the ego. The former was composed of two halves. The first half, the right mind told the Son, "You are Love and you never left Home." The second half, the wrong mind or the ego, said to him, "You killed God and can never return Home now", which created in him a sense of fear and guilt. This confused the Son and got him to start asking who was he and which way should he go? Which one should he believe: his wrong mind or his loving mind?

At this time, he was trying to figure out if he was Love or fear in this seemingly real dream and he was trying to remember his identity. In his confusion, the Son's ego tempted him to follow its reassuring guidance and the ego slowly gained his trust. The ego was the Son's creation and resides in the wrong-mind. It is only a thought made out of the guilt that resulted from when the Son believed that he had left God when he fell asleep. The ego is something apart from what God gave his Son and taught him. God and His Son are Love and happiness. Therefore, the ego and the mind are unreal because anything that is not made of Love is not from God and cannot exist. The Son forgot he was dreaming. But the more the Son played with the toy and pretended that it was real, the more it became real to him to the point where he forgot the toy was just part of a game. So the more power that he gave the ego, the more powerful it became in his mind.

As the Son began to believe that he had attacked his Source, he became terrified and the devious ego saw an opportunity to gain power over him. The ego presented itself as an ally to save the Son from his fear and advised him to look for a place to hide from a wrathful God who had returned from the dead and was looking to destroy his guilty Son.

While he was seeking refuge from his vengeful Father, the Son's ego advised him to hide in a place where his Father would never be able to find him.

The ego guided him to create a universe as his new, man-mad home that represented the opposite of God's Home of perfect Love and peace. This new universe was founded in fear, pain, anger, hate, jealousy, depression, anxiety, guilt, shame, blame, victimization, suffering—anything that doesn't feel good. Deceptively, the ego tricked the Son into believing that these things demonstrated the ego's false love for him and could replace God's perfect Love, but in fact, they ensured that he would never escape this universe of pain and suffering.

Now in listening to the ego's guidance, it made him falsely believe that he had actually conquered God and this made him feel omnipotent. The power went straight to his head and he became greedy. Suddenly in the dream, the power and greed felt soothing to him and comforted his insane mind. His ego self (THE ONE EGO) experienced the sense of power that came from pretending to create like his Father. It greatly enjoyed playing this game, and in his greediness he desired more toys to play with. The first set of ideas he manifested included other egos as people with separate identities, living separate lives in separate bodies. His ego created more toys, like different ethnicities, cultures, languages, nation-states, physical beauty, values, colors, money, homes, cars, clothes, fame, status, and objects that he could play with in his illusory dreamland. And each separate ego started to believe in the superficial peace and comfort that these objects and ideas seemed to offer him.

Still, he was also feeling guilty for leaving God although the Son forgot that it was only a dream. In actuality, the Son never left God but he couldn't remember his way back Home. Because of the guilt that the Son was experiencing, he created a whole host of sharp toys with which to punish himself that include fear, pain, suffering, anger, sadness, depression, hatred, jealousy, loneliness, boredom, confusion, and so on. Anything that doesn't feel good is of the ego and not who God's Son truly is. Yet, the Son treated these dangerous toys like a beloved baby blanket that he couldn't bear to lose. As he treasured and worshipped them, his memory of God, Heaven, and his true identity became more distant.

In his amnesia, the Son forgot that he was responsible for creating these negative toys in his life and so he blamed God and the other people for all that was wrong and fear-inducing in the universe. The Son's imagination was a gift from his Creator but he used its power against himself by creating fear guilt and projecting it outside of himself to keep him safe. Projection operates similar to the way a movie projector shows a film. Our thoughts and feelings are like the film on a reel that is shown through the movie projector and displayed on a screen that is our own separate universe. God is Love. That is why pain and suffering are not from God.

The son said since I'm creating everything in my life, then created sadness, pain and sufferings. That is when the ego developed and became stronger and stronger.

Since the Son is only dreaming of a world filled with bodies and forms, he's not actually here. He is still one spirit with God, sleeping next to his Creator and surrounded by angels in perfect safety. The ego knows this but tried to hide it from the Son because once he awakens from the dream, the ego will return to the nothingness from which it came.

Twenty

THE SEED AND THE HOLE

Returning to what I was guided to draw the night I was asking about who we are and where we came from, the black dot—the seed—I drew represented the moment we, as God's one Son, believed we left God in Heaven. When we left Him in our dream, we started out as a seed to taste a new life so we wrote a script to come and play in the land of physical experience and joyful thought (+&-). This script, manifested by our desire and imagination, became our seeming reality as the seed began to grow and split open. At this moment, we entered the playground of the universe with its toys of physical forms and duality so that we could experience contrasts and resistance.

As we wrote our stories, we were still programmed as Spirit to remember who we are as God's one Son in Heaven. Subconsciously, we understood that we were going to play and, in doing so, we were going to take on thousands of different roles in an infinite number of different dramas. But as soon as we left Home, we got wrapped up (invested) in our stories and took them very seriously. The illusory dream of birth and death only lasted a split second but because we experience it in slow motion, it appears very real. This means the process of life and death to time are not real.

In our forgetfulness, we became arrogant, selfish, and greedy. We got hooked on the power of co-creation, devising ever more self-defeating distractions, and became enamored with temptations. By doing this, we nurtured the idea of separation (from God and each other) and greed while not knowing that in the end, both were absolutely meaningless because it was all just a dream and nothing more. However the wrong-mind, the ego, tries to convince us that the opposite is true.

Thankfully, we've left ourselves clues and reminders in life to remember who we are. The memory of God still resides in our right mind with the Holy Spirit, which we could not completely extinguish. It symbolizes the part of the mind that was awakened before the seed came into being and reminds us that we are just playing in "life." These reminders appear everywhere in our daily lives and are the crumbs that will lead us back to our eternal life in God. For instance, when you plant a seed, it first sprouts curling roots and then a stem that reaches for the light. I noticed this with a plant I keep in my kitchen window and that I have to continually turn so that it will grow upright -because it keeps struggling to go to the light. This is a little reminder that we left within our lives to say, "This is who you are. Go back to the light." The light will tell you who you are, but we have become so distracted with fear and anxiety that we forget which way we must go to reach the light. But if you keep watering the seed, it will continue to grow towards the light. Between the right mind and the wrong is the decision-maker of the dream that is our true Spirit.

Twenty-One

The Mind

One day while I was meditating, unexpectedly, brilliant physicist Albert Einstein showed me a bubble that symbolized the universe that we create with our thoughts and emotions. He shared with me that it appears big and spacious inside the bubble/universe and it also seems solid and real. Hence we believe that we're getting somewhere with our achievements and material gains in this universe, but they're not connected to the Infinite Power of our Spirit. The man-made universe is filled with external temptations and conditional love that lead us to dead ends, where we feel trapped in an endless maze of chaos. It's like a merry-go-round or a boomerang—what goes around comes around. So whatever you're thinking and feeling, that thought and felling will come back to you.

Building on Einstein's message, in a second meditation days later, I saw a 12-year-old boy standing inside a bubble, I felt that it was myself. He raised his hands up over his head and poked his fingertips through the top of the bubble to make an opening. When he lifted his arms, I saw him smiling; he was so happy and excited to be setting himself free and finding more to explore. In doing this, he invited Love, Light, Faith, and Trust into his thoughts.

By choosing the loving mind he was leaving behind his chaotic thoughts. He was present and aware of his feelings, thoughts and, in turn, built a stronger foundation for Inner Love to reach the stars and his own Godly Power.

It is with both our foundation and our decision-making that we create our own man-made universe; the home of our creation. Specifically, we learn who to be and how to fit in while forming our beliefs and values. Consequently, we are the designer and the builder. We engineered every little detail to build this universe.

Yet, as children we are taught about the universe being this mysterious place that contains countless galaxies and stars, which are physically light-years away from us. We are told this enigmatic universe holds the answers to the beginning of time, space, and life. Little do we know that the universe is within each of us, not without. It is in our minds, our emotions, thoughts, and our beliefs. This means you are the god of your own creations. You made every object, every event, and every situation that you experience with your thoughts and imagination, including your body, pain, suffering, sadness, happiness, joy, and life lessons. It is all about your beliefs and what you are inviting into your mind because what you think (ideas and beliefs) is what you fill up your universe with.

As long as we are in the physical body, we never stop feeling and paving life (thinking) and creating experiences. By choosing the loving mind, you are aware of your fearful chaotic thoughts. Be present and stay grateful for all of your thoughts and, in turn, build a strong foundation for the Truth of who You are in the Universe of Unconditional Love.

the universe = home of all our creations

Twenty-Two

How to Check the Pulse
of Unconscious Thoughts

---

*Becoming aware of all of our conscious and
unconscious pulsing thoughts will enable us to gain
our freedom from the web of stressful thinking.*

Our journey to peace requires us to take command of our emotions, feelings, thoughts, decision-making, and creations. In order to take the first step along this path, we need to become aware of all of our thoughts. As we learned earlier, our pulsing emotions and thoughts create our reality, but where do these thoughts come from? Our thoughts are the source or by-product of the culmination of our old habits and beliefs with which we have been programmed. Those thoughts could either imprison us in pain and suffering and hold us hostage, or bring us Inner Peace. Consequently, we need to become the gatekeeper of all our beliefs, thoughts, and emotions and take responsibility for our choices.

Let's try this now by entering together into the Lab of Consciousness. On a sheet of paper, as you are sitting quietly, write down 10 or more thoughts.

Do not be selective as your thoughts come. Put down anything that comes to mind, regardless of how trivial or silly it seems.

1. Today is a beautiful day.
2. I hate my job.
3. How am I going to pay my bills this month?
4. I'm tired.
5. I'm hungry.
6. I love this book.
7. I'm excited to go on vacation.
8. I love my dogs.
9. I have to make a phone call.
10. Did I lock the front door?

Now that you have written down at least 10 thoughts, look at them carefully. You will place all of your positive thoughts—anything that brings you to the state of joy and makes you feel good (your GPS) by thinking about it—in the Universe of Love on your sheet. All negative thoughts, doubts, questions, such as "I have to yawn," "I need to scratch my toe," "I am frustrated," or "I am tired," do not go in the Universe of Love.

Universe of Love

In the example above, the numbers shown in the Universe represent positive feelings and thoughts while the others still need to be disciplined. The goal is to eventually put all of your thoughts in the circle.

The Group of the Fatherhood shared this tool with me to empower individuals by becoming aware of their thoughts. In other words, be aware of what comes in and what goes out (train your mind to be the gatekeeper of your thoughts). The key is to not just focus on what consciously comes to mind (pretending to be positive). This is because the subconscious mind holds all of our beliefs, habits, experiences, memories, values, stories, and myths. Together they comprise the foundation of our thoughts. Their impact is often outside of our conscious awareness, yet they are very powerful in guiding and directing our current emotions, feelings, thoughts, perceptions, attitudes, preferences, decisions, reactions, and behavior. Thus, becoming aware of all of our conscious and unconscious pulsing thoughts will enable us to gain our freedom from the web of stressful thinking.

beliefs → emotions → thoughts

How long you need to continue practicing this exercise depends on you. If any thought does not come from your loving mind (feeling good), as you go through your day, you are not yet done practicing. Any thoughts you hold disconnected from love come from fear. So use this exercise every day, anytime, anywhere, and for any situation. Just carry a small notebook and a pen with you or type a memo in your cell phone.

Be patient as life is full of yummy surprises! I know you will get there because I, along with many others, have tasted the deliciousness that stems from consistently using this tool. I am not telling you that life is full of joy all the time. If you are experiencing something that is unpleasant, know that you have a choice since there are always other ways to look at the situation and lessons to learn from it. What you need to do is be aware of your emotions and your thoughts because, when you are present, you are selective. In the present moment, you can sift through your thoughts like panning for gold nuggets, so that when a thought feels good, you bring it out and keep it. Such positive thinking will lead you along your bright and clear path.

<u>*Notes*</u>

Twenty-Three

Operating on Automatic (Programming)

---

*We perceive ourselves as victims
due to our old beliefs, emotions, and thoughts.*

So now we know that the contents of the subconscious mind (our foundation) are driving our thinking. We are then unconsciously operating on autopilot and unaware from where our thoughts and emotions are coming. This happens because we have been programmed to choose fearful thinking and thus become a hostage to our fear-based thoughts. Trapped in the fearful part of our mind (the logical mind or the ego), we hop, skip, and jump and automatically choose a thought that does not feel good. The hostage crisis results because we have forgotten our True Identity, and now we believe what we think and do with the fearful part of our mind.

We perceive ourselves as victims due to our old beliefs, emotions, and thoughts.

**choosing the thought of fear + panic = fear of darkness
old thought + old habits→ belief + values of a victim**

Let us take a closer look at how we come to believe in myths and illusions, which is actually a look at how our foundation is formed. My Teachers told me that our fear-based programming began millions of years ago (and is still pulsing now) At the time, we were living in caves and we did not have clothes, food, or any formal schooling. We had nothing. We survived by hunting for food and our way of living was simple. No one cried for anything and suddenly, by accident, somebody started crying and making noise. Someone else sensed the sadness in those tears, and so we made tears to express our grief and sorrow. Crying was then associated with our sadness, as we started to give meaning to things.

Similarly, during that time, someone smiled and showed their teeth, and we felt a happy feeling. We then programmed a specific behavior—smiling— to show our happiness. Long story short, we programmed ourselves based on what someone else did by choosing to copy their behavior in order to fit in, which today we call conforming to peer pressure.

Over the years, we programmed many different behaviors and actions, not knowing there are other ways to think and act. We mindlessly go along with what our upbringing, family, culture, and experiences teach us in a sleepwalking state. Sleepwalking in this case is defined as being disconnected from Love and the Power within us.

In this state, we unknowingly pick fearful thoughts as our god and unquestioningly obey its orders. Deep down we know that these thoughts are not true, yet since we assembled them we can also disassemble them by changing our mind, or remembering the Truth. We will cover how to disassemble our miscreation's in Chapter Seven on deprogramming.

Our obedience to fear disconnects us from who we Truly are as Love and reinforces our false belief that we now must look for Love outside of ourselves. There are several consequences for seeking Love without, including depression, loneliness, guilt, victimization, and so on. Feelings of discomfort indicate that we are unaware of what we are thinking and this happens when we are not present.

Moreover, in being disconnected from the loving mind we see all of our problems, regardless of their size, as overwhelming and we struggle to try and solve them. In turn, we invite more fear into our space and this fear makes the challenges in our thoughts seem very real and complicated. Our disconnection leads to more thoughts that create more problems in a chain effect of chaos. As a result, we feel trapped in an endless maze of hopelessness and darkness.

In reality, our experiences are not problems if we are present and aware of what comes into our mind, what is hidden in the subconscious, and what goes out. They are life lessons and there is a gift in each challenge that will lead us to the Inner Peace that we all are seeking. By being present and aware of our thoughts, this awareness will bring us the willingness to invite miracles into our lives.

If we choose to view every situation as a life lesson rather than a problem and bravely open up the present (to detox guilt), the fear will disappear and make a Doorway to Peace. Choosing to acknowledge and walk through that Doorway is a miracle.

pain + suffering → signal (a lesson from which to learn)
love + joy + peace + happiness = the loving mind and loving heart
open heart = loving mind

Twenty-Four

EMBARKING ON OUR EXPRESSWAY

The Power is within you, and now you know where to go to find the answers to all of your questions in life, your Altar (Heart).

As we discussed in the last chapter, the foundation of all of our thoughts and emotions are based on our beliefs, habits, past experiences, values, and myths accumulated in this lifetime and in our past lives. Our foundation directs not only our current thoughts but also subconsciously directs our decision-making.

When we are facing our foundation, we have to look at our past and ask ourselves if these thoughts and stories are true anymore. Do these thoughts help or hinder us in making decisions in life? Our fearful beliefs and stories can cloud our vision and cast shadows and doubts. They build a barrier between us and our peace of mind.

Here is a very simple but powerful example illustrating how our old beliefs and stories can be rendered powerless to bring us peace of mind. I encounter many people who struggle with their body image. Initially unsure how to approach the subject, because it is a sensitive issue for most people, I requested guidance from my Teachers in explaining how the mind is actually in charge of the physical body and not the other way around.

A specific message immediately came to me for one individual. I told her to look at her toe, and I then asked if her toe tells her how to feel. She quieted down for a second and a big smile of relief spread across her face, as she answered no.

Continuing on, I told her that now she knows her body is not in charge, her thinking mind is. Her body is not telling her how to feel, her thoughts are. By changing her mind and thus her story, she could direct her body in how to be, how to feel, and how to look.

While we were talking, I also saw in my mind's eye the image shown below, which the Group instructed me to share with her and others. The accompanying tool will guide us through any challenges, decisions, or confusions in life by helping us achieve a clear mind and clear thoughts and emotions. Being in charge (aware) of our thoughts and emotions will take us to The Expressway to Clarity that runs between the mind and the heart.

Expressway to Clarity

On top, we find the mind – filled with thoughts, both loving and fearful. The mind is forever pulsing and vibrating, and thereby creating.

Below is the heart, where our emotions, feelings, and intuition act as our very powerful GPS—or guidance system—in life. I see this as our Lab of Emotions in which we experience all kinds of different feelings. For example, when you feel happy, your heart is in a balanced rhythm and excited in a positive and peaceful way. You then know that the decision you are making is the right way to go because that good feeling is gratifying and is what we are constantly searching for: the feeling of peace; freedom; and abundance (the remembrance of who we are). These are our true gut feelings to which we should pay attention. On the other hand, when you feel fearful, your heart starts pounding in distress. It is telling you that you are experiencing feelings foreign to your Spirit (not of love) and that the decision you are making is not the way to go. You need to change your direction, as you are learning your life lessons through the eyes of love.

Between the mind and the heart (emotions), we find the expressway – forever connecting our emotions and internalized knowledge with our outward-focused, conscious thoughts. It is this pathway that provides the key to harmony in our lives.

The Lab of Emotions

Close your eyes to minimize any distractions. Go within your heart and feel something you experienced in life that brought you a happy and joyful feeling. Go to that space—the Point of Simplicity—and feel the love. It could come from holding a newborn baby, cuddling your pets, or even tasting a bite of your favorite food; whatever brings you to that space of love.

Stop, close your eyes, go within, play, and practice. Now take a deep breath and open your eyes. How did you feel?

Your emotions are the key to the Infinite Power of your mind. You can use this process of getting in touch with your feelings to quickly answer any questions that you have in life and to guide your decision-making.

The Experimental Lab

So let us experiment and create in The Lab some more. You have to connect your mind to your heart and your heart to your mind. If you stay only in the mind and ask a question, your logical thoughts will tell you what to do but they may not lead you to the right decision. However, when you connect to your gut feelings, you find out what you really want.

We can practice this simple and quick tool right now. First, ask yourself a question, like something you want to do today but you are not sure about it. Ask yourself and do not stay in your head. Drive down the expressway, and then listen and see how you feel. Connect that question to your heart, where you can feel it.

Take a deep breath. If you want to close your eyes you can and if not that is fine, too. Now ask that question. Let the question be. Do not try to solve it, analyze it, or ignore it. Stay out of your own way, out of your head, and invite your feelings to come to the forefront. This exercise can be done literally in seconds; the length of time it takes you to inhale and exhale once in a relaxed manner.

Now come out of it. How did you feel about the question you asked?

1. If you felt good about it, that is the right decision. It means yes, do it.
2. If you felt worried or anxious, your feelings are telling you no. It means do not do it.
3. If you felt unsure, any doubt, or uncertainty, it means you have reached a stop sign, and you need to take your time and be patient. Your feelings are telling you to wait, be still, and meditate on the answer rather than trying to analyze or solve it with your logical mind.

The Expressway will help you connect to your feelings, and your feelings would not lie to you unless you ignore them. For example, when we are happy, no one can tell us that we are not because we know for sure we are happy. The awareness of our feelings will lead us to make the right decisions since we can trust that our loving thoughts are our best friends. In contrast, would you trust the guidance of someone you are afraid of or not comfortable with? That is precisely what our fearful thoughts are. This is why it is so important to be present and be aware of what come into our minds; to be aware of our choices and see if they are serving us. Then we will not be caught off-guard and get blindsided.

So if you are experiencing any confusion in your life, like whether you should change jobs, get married, or have children, you do not need to search outside of yourself for guidance. It takes time but start out by using this tool for little things, such as choosing coffee or tea or deciding what to eat, and then move onto bigger questions. It is very easy. All you have to do is practice, and be sure to balance it with common sense. The Power is within you, and now you know where to go to find the answers to all of your questions in life: your Altar.

<u>*Notes*</u>

Twenty-Five

THE MAN-MADE UNIVERSE

---

*By choosing the loving mind, you leave behind
your fearful and chaotic thoughts.*

Up to this point we have covered the process of creating with the pulsing thoughts in our mind, the foundation of our thoughts, and the way to make decisions using our emotions and feelings. It is with both our foundation and decision-making that we create our own universe—the man-made universe—home of our creations. Specifically, I am referring to the creation of our own lives and lifestyles, as we learn who to be, and how to fit in, while forming our beliefs and values. Consequently, we are the designer and the builder. We engineered every little detail to build this universe with our thoughts.

Yet, as children we were taught about the universe being this mysterious place that contains countless galaxies and stars, which are physically light-years away from us. We are told this enigmatic universe holds the answers to the beginning of time, space, and life. Little do we know that the universe is within each of us, not without. It is in our minds: our thoughts and beliefs. This means you are the god of your own creations. You make every object, every event, and every situation that you experience with your thoughts, imagination, and your body: pain, suffering, sadness, happiness, joy, and life lessons. It is all about your beliefs and what you are inviting into your mind because what you think (ideas and beliefs) is what you fill up your universe with.

As long as we are in the physical body, we never stop pulsing (thinking) and creating more thoughts and experiences. In addition, whatever you are thinking will be reflected back to you and create more of the same, like a boomerang: what goes around comes back around.

By choosing the loving mind, you leave behind your fearful and chaotic thoughts. Be present and stay grateful for all of your thoughts, and in turn, build a strong foundation for the Truth of who You are in the Universe of Unconditional Love (God).

Let us get to know your universe at this present moment.

the universe = home of all our creations (our stage)

The Universe of the ThinkTank

Steps:

1. Stand up and stretch your arms out straight.
2. Imagine a circle all around you that extends as far as your fingertips can reach in all directions. Your circle reaches up over your head, below your feet, and all around you. This is the size of your universe.
3. See yourself in the center of your universe.

4. Now ask yourself, "with what kind of thoughts am I filling up my universe?"
5. Am I joyful?
6. Am I fearful?
7. Do I feel the expansion of Love?
8. Or do I feel suffocated?
9. Ask yourself, "What if I am the god of my own universe? What would I fill up my universe with? Love or fear?"
10. Face whatever you have made in your universe.
11. Whatever you are thinking and filling up your universe with right now is your foundation. Is it positive or negative? Happy or sad?
12. The thoughts you think are the building blocks of your universe.

13. Bravely weed out the fearful thoughts from your universe by facing them.

14. When you face your fearful thoughts, you learn the lessons from your experiences. In gaining this knowledge, you disempower the fear of darkness and are gradually led to the Light.

15. By choosing the Light, your universe will shine and glow with Love.

16. By choosing Love, you merge your universe with those of others, thereby joining in <u>One</u>ness.

17. How do you feel at this present moment? If you feel happy, your universe is filled with happy thoughts. If not, it is okay to feel suffocated because the restriction will bring you the awareness of its opposite. Look behind the challenge and turn it around to make a brighter universe, bringing more Clarity into your life.

Personal Blueprint

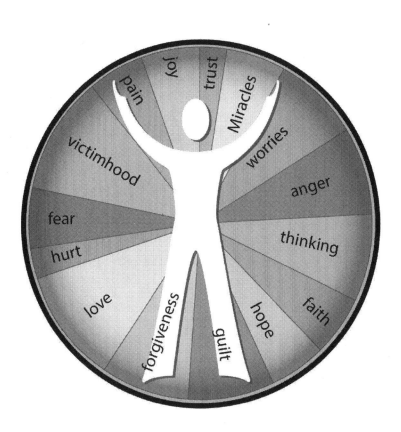

Everyone has a different blueprint for their universe, depending on the type of thoughts, beliefs, and values they hold. So let us imagine your universe filled with loving thoughts.

When you connect to love, the Light of joy and happiness casts a beautiful glow all around your universe that expands to reach more loving Light. The more you choose Unconditional Love, the more you fearlessly poke through the edge of your own true universe (the Gate of Light) to join with the universes of others. Your willingness to open the gate of light will bring clarity (Knowledge) to reach one another. By choosing to see the Truth and expanding your light, the quicker you reach the state of <u>One</u>ness with God.

Clarity to See the Truth in Your ThinkTank

Universe of Oneness

Gate of Light + expansion of love → <u>Oneness</u>

The expansion of love will take you through the Portal of Light to the Home of Unconditional Love, where you merge into <u>Oneness</u> with God (Home, Sweet Home). Here you are Whole and Complete and nothing else, meaning there is no separation or barriers to Love.

The Portal of Light – One with God

Now imagine you are filling up your universe with fear, pain, and suffering. You will see the world upside-down. As you are looking at your life from this confused point of view, your fearful thoughts generate more fear.

When you get turned upside-down, you cannot think nor see straight and thus build a wall of fear (darkness) around your universe that blocks the Light and Clarity. This wall reinforces your sense of isolation and separation from the Source (Unconditional Love), which leads to depression.

isolation + separation → depression

The darkness also impedes your ability to make decisions with your loving mind, and so you choose to play with the sharp toys of the logical mind - anything that is not of love, such as fear, shame, blame, guilt, hate, pain, loneliness, suffering, anger, judgment, confusion, special relationships, neediness, attachments, victimization, gossip, alcohol, drugs, etc. In playing with sharp toys, you are trying to find light in darkness, peace in fear, which is impossible (and a form of insanity).

Wall of fear + darkness = sharp toys (a fearful attitude)
sharp toys = hate + judgment
peace + fear = insanity

The light will not turn on because Love does not know about fear. To make a brighter universe and to reach peace, we have to de-clutter all of our fears.

This is the process of seeing the Truth behind the insane thoughts that we create and with which we fill up our universe. When we are willing to let go of our past and learn the lessons from our creations (clear the wall of fear), we release pain and suffering and the doors open up to welcome the light of Love. The only thing we have to do is bravely invite our life experiences in and look at each one of them with their own special color (message) without any judgment.

It is no different than trying anything novel in life, for instance, tasting a new food. We take it so seriously when we do not like something, yet we can be grateful for the experience. This food example applies to anything in life: a new relationship, job, environment or sad moment. When we look at the situation and learn our lesson from it, that is a miracle (a shift in perception), and the miracle will start the process of forgiveness - to give and see love in all of our experiences.

In turn, we come to realize that they are simply our experiences and we are just trying something, so we will not give them power. As long as we know that we are here to experience our miscreation, but we are not of them, they are not going to hurt us. It is the same thing as being in this world, but not of it. As a result, we can abolish the wall of fear, invite light into our universe, and then reach out and join in <u>Oneness</u>.

awareness + life lessons = forgiveness

On the other hand, when we shift our thinking to darkness (thinking with the ego), our awareness is shut off and our decision-making becomes impaired, meaning that we forget we are the masters of our universe (our thinking mind). When we lose that connection, we are disempowered and our disempowerment produces more fearful thoughts that continue on and expand to more dark thoughts, like the coils on a slinky connecting one thought after another. As we stretch out the slinky, each fearful thought takes us farther and farther away from who we Truly are. In this case, fear gives birth to a baby that grows, and in turn, produces more offspring that are nurtured and programmed in darkness and isolation.

The thoughts of the slinky can also be visualized as pulses in the mind. The mind produces high beats and low beats, based on the kind of thoughts we are thinking. By monitoring (building our awareness of) the beats—or pulse—we will be guided to make different choices, similar to how we used The Expressway to Clarity.

The pulsations of fear from the logical mind (the ego) are unconscious (automatic) and produce more of the same in our universe, as shown below in the slinky diagram. However, the high pulse of fearful thoughts can make us aware of our emotions and feelings, and lead us to look for the lesson in our fearful experiences (be friends with our fear).

The low pulse of Joyfulness and Inner Peace (operating manually and in stillness) will guide us to choose the loving mind, as we are focusing on and making positive thoughts that infuse more peace in our universe.

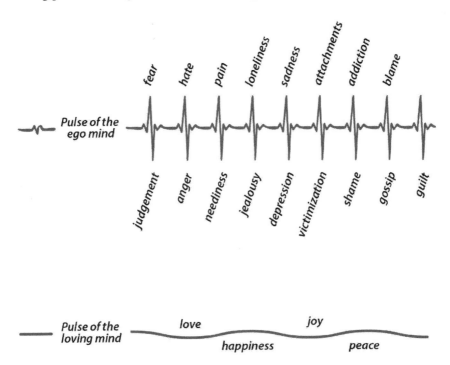

The key is: when you are not present, do not invite these strangers (the painful thoughts) in. Our fearful thoughts are not welcome, and we need to be selective of what comes in and what goes out. By being present and aware of our thoughts, we can be kinder to ourselves and others in a more prosperous way. Together we can design a healthier universe more efficiently. Here, we can make beautiful experiences and this beauty will expand into everything that is whole and complete.

With this knowledge of our Self, we can easily avoid faulty, unnecessary choices. Choose only thoughts that bring you to the messages of clarity (the Oneness with God).

Note

Twenty-Six

SHIFTING TO MANUAL (DEPROGRAMMING)

Be fearless and trust your Inner Guidance and selfless Love.

We just learned how we create our own universe, based on our thoughts, beliefs, and values. We also learned how we have been programmed over time in how to think and act, disconnecting us from the Love that we are. Here now are two methods to gently and lovingly deprogram—or disassemble—our fearful beliefs and values to reach Inner Peace and to reconnect with who we Truly are.

Before using them, first we have to be present to reach the conscious mind, and second, go deeper to the contents stored in our subconscious mind. Third, we must be willing to bring them to the surface. Be fearless and trust your Inner Guidance and selfless Love.

Method 1 - Erasing Fearful Beliefs

As noted earlier, well before we are born our minds are carrying beliefs and values from the past in our subconscious. Then when we learn the beliefs, habits, values, and myths of the collective in the present, they also become imprinted on us. In other words, we are programmed with these beliefs to fit into society. By the time we are a little older, we have been brainwashed by ancient, fear-based beliefs, values, and thoughts, and accordingly, we perceive everything through the lens of judgment.

My Teachers told me that to wash away all of these old beliefs and values, we have to erase everything in the fearful mind and start all over. Next, they showed me a sheet of paper. They wanted me to play with the paper as a movie screen. The Group then explained that we are pretending it's a movie screen, and whatever we write on the sheet we project onto the screen. By erasing what is written on that piece of paper from the logical mind, we are washing away our fearful beliefs and insane thoughts. It may not be easy but it is a choice. Think of it as giving away your old clothes and belongings that you no longer want.

STEPS:

1. First, you have to be willing to acknowledge your ancient beliefs and values. Some examples of these are: I am unworthy and unlovable; I need a partner to feel loved and secure; I must take care of everyone else before myself; and my self-worth is determined by my career and status.
2. Be willing to question all of the beliefs and values that you hold.
3. Get a sheet of paper, a pencil, and an eraser.
4. Write down all of your beliefs and values. Example: Your value is determined by your education level. (This may hold true but only for the subject matter in which you are being educated.)
5. Look them over for the last time.
6. Now take an eraser and erase everything you wrote down on that sheet of paper. You are erasing away all of your old beliefs, with an open mind for a fresh start.

By deprogramming, you are starting your new journey, like a newborn baby (playing with Joy rather than judgment and receiving guidance from pure

Love). This will not happen overnight. It is a gradual process that takes time and dedication.

The purpose of this tool is to show you that all of your old beliefs and values are not necessarily true for you anymore. They come from judgment, which does not feel good since it reinforces separation. Now you will be aware of new ways of thinking. You will be making your own beliefs and values without fearful thoughts of others being injected into your thinking that block you from reaching peace. As a result, you empower yourself to build the life that you desire. You will be your own master. Mastery comes from your willingness, and it occurs when you are present and aware of all of your thoughts.

ancient beliefs + ancient values = judgment
releasing fear + being present → mastery

Method 2 - Sheet in the Wind

Here is the second way to experience our creation and to deprogram to reach Inner Peace. This tool illustrates three different ways to look at our life experiences. My teachers wanted me to share the information with the group, and the details of the tool were revealed as follows:

Scenario #1: Imagine you are a white linen sheet hanging up on a clothesline. Suddenly, a strong wind comes and you, as the sheet, become very fearful. You cling to the only thing you have known. You are absolutely terrified and struggle against the situation. You ask yourself, "Why me? What should I do?" You are overwhelmed with stress, panic-stricken, and feeling victimized. From that point on, you feel depressed because you perceive the wind (your life experiences) as a tragedy rather than a life lesson. When you give your power away to other people and situations, you remain disempowered and this is when you experience illness and disease.

fear + panic = victimization
fear + anxiety = wakeup call

Scenario #2: Imagine you are a white sheet hanging up on a clothesline. Suddenly, a strong wind comes. As you notice the wind approaching, you become angry and fearful. You kick and scream, and you fight so hard that the wind grabs you off the clothesline. While the wind carries you away, it throws you against the rocks and trees, destroying you with the power of fear, hate, and anger. In being violently tossed about, the sheet rips and tears and shreds into small pieces. This is when you give your life away and get destroyed by your fearful thoughts.

why me? + poor me! = victimization
scream + fight = fear

Scenario #3: Imagine you are a white sheet hanging up on a clothesline. Suddenly, a strong wind comes. As you notice the wind approaching, you become so happy and playful. You perceive this as a beautiful time to sing and dance with joy and happiness, as you are brushing your hair with the wind. While singing and dancing, the wind carries your voice across the whole universe and soothes and brightens everyone's heart.

joy + beauty = dancing with peace

The purpose of this last exercise is to show you that when you have faith and trust the music of Heaven will never stop playing. The Music is constantly playing, but we are not tuned in to hear it when our feelings of victimization distract us. As you choose to hear the Music of Love or fear, Peace or anger, Joy or sadness, Clarity or darkness, it will empower you to go with the flow of life and sing with any situation since everything you are experiencing is coming from your beliefs, values, and thoughts.

There is a great lesson in every life experience, and you just have to remember that nothing can abolish and destroy who You Truly are. Anything that comes from fear, anger, and judgment may destroy your peace of mind and perhaps even your body, but by using this tool you can gain back your

Power and perceive Peace and Joy that you can expand (project) to others. The more you recognize that you are Peace, the more you offer It and the more you receive It.

The remembrance of and Faith in God + Clarity of all lessons = Peace
Love + projection = giving and receiving love
You + God = <u>Oneness</u>

Notes

Twenty-Seven

EXPRESS ROUTES

Unwrapping the gift of fear will lead you to the state of Hope.

Now as you are getting to know who You are, you are ready to make use of tools that can help you build your foundation on solid ground. So when you encounter any challenges in life, no storm will knock you down and nothing will obliterate you because nothing can destroy Love. Love is the truth of who You are, and no one can take that away from you.

Recall that earlier we saw how we could use a simple cotton ball to remind us to be gentle and weightless. The techniques that follow will help you monitor the thoughts that come into your mind, set you free from fearful thinking, and enable you to bring more peace into your universe. Being aware of what comes into your thoughts (joy or fear) and holding onto a little willingness might be exhausting, but never give up. If you are willing to take charge of your thinking, these tools will help you to stay present.

I. *Bubbly Thoughts*

This tool came to me at the same time as the universe message, which I shared earlier, to show how we can be playful with our thoughts rather than letting them take control of our lives.

Imagine, while blowing bubbles, that you are watching children play and dance. The children teach you that your fearful thoughts are hollow, like bubbles. Know that their seeming weight is only in your mind.

We are here to play with duality, and every loving and fearful thought has its own beauty and color that represents different life experiences and lessons. As long as you know who You Truly are and that your Inheritance is God's Love, you have nothing to fear. Love will melt all fearful thoughts.

ROAD MAP:

1. Get a bottle of blowing bubbles and begin to blow the bubbles into the air.
2. At this time, be aware of your thoughts and see each one as a bubble. It could be either a happy or stressful thought.
3. As you blow the bubbles, noting that each captures your thoughts, look at their color and size. See the bubbles the way a child sees them with joyful, innocent eyes.

   In order to be joyful and to reach the vision of innocence, you have to be aware of the lessons. As you are watching your fearful thoughts, see the lessons within them to set you free of suffering. If it is difficult to do, know that what is behind the fear is actually love. Allow the fearful thoughts to transform into the playfulness of the floating bubbles.
4. Begin playing and dance with them; they will bring you the Music of Joy. Fearlessly poke (do not be afraid to look within the thoughts) and kick (release and surrender) them. Pretend they are your playmates.
5. As more thoughts come, blow more bubbles and release them.

This tool will build your awareness of all of your thoughts. It reminds you to not take life so seriously and to play and dance with all of your thoughts.

II. Hand Clench

This tool will help you to be aware of your stressful thoughts and to quickly release them. It can be used while you are at work, showering, exercising, or watching a movie. You can do this anywhere, at any time, in any circumstance.

STEPS:

1. Close your eyes and breathe calmly. Invite the Divine into your heart.
2. Next, hold your hands, palms facing upwards, in a clenched position (making a fist). They must be completely closed.
3. Now imagine you are putting all of your thoughts of worry, stress, and pain into your clenched hands.
4. Take a few minutes to fill them up.
5. Are your hands beginning to feel heavy?
6. Now take a deep breath, raise your clenched hands up level with your heart, and slowly open them.
7. Imagine all of your stress and worries are fading away in the Light of the Divine, as His Unconditional Love purifies them.
8. Now quickly close and open your hands several times, and imagine and feel the weightlessness that comes from releasing all of your stress.

III. Wind Release

Here is a tool that I discovered, while out for a walk one day. I heard the wind blowing through the trees, rustling the leaves and whistling between the branches. It sounded very relaxing, as it was coming and going. Suddenly, I received a message from my Teachers:

Imagine, as you are facing the wind, that you can release all of your worries by letting them go into the air and set yourself free from their burden.

You are shedding all of your negative thoughts and stress.

While you are releasing them in the wind, you feel refreshed, bright, and weightless once more.

Accept that the wind is here to carry the load for you. Do not go against the wind by engaging in judgment or doubt (see the lessons in all of your experiences). Just like you never question where the wind comes from, have Trust and fearlessly release your worries.

You can do this at the beach, when you take a walk outside, or even in front of a fan. It might sound silly or overly simple, but it works.

You can say this out loud or quietly. Just Be with the wind and release. Take your time.

1. Imagine all of the stress and madness loosening from you one by one. They go up to the sky, where your guardian angel collects and dissolves them for you (guides you through the process of forgiveness).
2. As you continue repeating this tool, imagine this is your first day on earth. Start making more joyful experiences through your Divine Power of co-creation. And always know that God's Love is in your thoughtful creations (your whole universe is filled with Love).

I V. *Disciplining Fear and Anxiety*

My Teachers introduced me to this tool when I was helping a severely depressed client. While I was working with her, I could intuitively and physically feel her depression and anxiety. As her heart was pounding, mine began to pound, too. The pain was so intense that it felt as though my chest was exploding.

Being with her in this dark hole, I understood that it is an overwhelming challenge for people to guide themselves through all of the darkness and through all of the painful thoughts that come into their minds. I asked my Teachers, "How do I get out of this confused state of mind?" They answered:

Here is a simple, yet very powerful, approach that will help you when you have confused, dark thoughts and when you get turned upside-down in your universe. You can use this tool every day to ground yourself.

Following their instructions, the Group led my client and me to the light of peace at the end of the tunnel. Before embarking on this exercise, be sure to get plenty of rest and eat properly to receive the full benefits. We are programmed such that we need adequate sleep and nourishment otherwise we become exhausted and drained. That is when the ego takes over and life seems really difficult.

When this happens, do not give up. Do not fall into the trap of fear. It feels real, but it is not actually there. When you get over-tired, you have to be very, very gentle with yourself. For this reason, you can keep repeating the following steps, particularly since it will take time to deprogram your thoughts as you have been programmed over many lifetimes.

ROAD MAP:

1. **Be aware of your emotions**
   - In disciplining fear and anxiety, remember to look behind what you are feeling to see its opposite: love and joy. Love and Joy are who You are. Know that fear and anxiety have no power over you because they are not who You are.

2. **Drink water**
   - Get yourself a glass of spring water and while you are drinking, imagine the water washing away all of your fear and anxiety.

3. **Breathe fresh air**
   - Keep drinking the water and sit in or observe the outdoors; being in nature and the fresh air is very powerful. Breathe and trust that God is here with you in your breath (it is like an umbilical cord) the same way you trust that your breath will always bring you more life.

- As you are breathing, your breath will bring you to the present moment and that is where Love Is. The present moment has nothing to do with time; it is the remembrance of God.

4. **Pray**
    - Now ask God to walk with you at all times, to help you not judge, and to show you what Unconditional Love Is. Ask Him to guide you Peace and Clarity.
    - Pray without any fear or neediness. Do not pray for things, such as a new house or to win the lottery.

V. White Egg

While working on this book I have thought about fear and why we give it so much power. I have wondered why fear feels so real and in response, my Teachers have offered more tools with which to play. At one point, they showed me a white egg to illustrate what fear is made of, then said:

This egg provides a great way to see how fragile fear actually is and how beneficial it is to experience fear.

Everyone is taught to be fearful, fragile, and sensitive. By using this tool, it will help you experience your fear in new and exciting ways.

Now here is the Road Map they shared with me:

1. Hold a white egg in your hands.
2. See the egg as a fearful situation that you are facing at this present moment or any fear that you have in life right now, from the past, or about the future.
3. Break the eggshell by tapping it, squeezing it, or dropping it in front of you and watch it (to face and release your fear).

4. Dive into the fear. Experiencing that fear will help you reach the gate-way to more clarity and light. When you face it, the fear will disappear and the doors of opportunity will open.

5. Note how fragile your fear is. In experiencing and facing it, you can now enjoy the abundance accompanying fear (the egg white and yolk, your life lessons). Most people are afraid to face their fear though. If you hide from it, your fear (eggs) will gain power and hatch chicks that breed more of the same (fear). However, if you face the fear, it will lose its power and vanish.

Facing the abundance found in fear—or any unpleasant situation—will bring you the awareness of Peace. If you know that pain and suffering are a gift (a miracle), it will help you forgive any situation in life. Unwrapping that gift of fear will lead you to the state of Hope.

VI. Road Signs of Hope

There are many messages in the physical world that can free you from your complicated thoughts, such as the beauty and simplicity found in nature. Nature and animals possess clues that when you discover them, like Indiana Jones, provide you with a map to reach greater Inner Peace (home, sweet home) and reconnect you to the true nature of who You are. The mothering and nurturing guidance of nature will help you discipline your thoughts and empower you through its loving, joyful, and hopeful messages.

When you are out in nature, notice how you feel energized with love, refreshed, and peaceful. As you are present and share your love with nature, it will love you back. You feel that <u>One</u>ness, and through your direct connection it will speak to you.

Here is one of my favorite messages that a tree once shared with me in the wintertime:

Look at me standing tall, strong, and beautiful, overcoming all obstacles. I have no clothes on (leaves), not even undergarments. I am not giving up, and the only thing I have left is Hope for spring.

I am going with the flow of time and space, and I am willing to let the past, the future, and all attachments go. I release and surrender to the laws of the physical world.

This tree's story represents that of all trees, as they stand with pride, fearlessly saying, "Here I am, winter. Come to me." They never complain that it is cold, even in the freezing wind. They never fuss that they are bare-naked because they still remember who they are, standing so powerfully. The only thing they have—that no one can take away—is Hope. They have Hope that spring is coming, the leaves will bloom, and the fruit will grow.

The trees would suffer if they demanded, "I want leaves now! I want to be pretty, green, and abundantly fruitful right now!" Nothing positive would come from these stressful thoughts. Not surprisingly, the trees would become stressed and diseased, imprison themselves in their thoughts, and drain themselves to death.

When you feel stressed, look at the trees outside. Pay attention to their quiet calm and stillness both in the wintry, dark, cold night and in the blazing sun (hardship). We can be the same way. Whatever is happening in your life, use inspiration from the trees. Hope will help you learn to be patient, while you undergo the process of shifting your perception of your life experiences. Ultimately, Hope is the mother of patience.

Breathe hope from the trees into your lungs and breathe out the gift of appreciation that is Love. Hope and Love will come when you are 100% sure of, and have faith and trust in, who You are.

VII. Day and Night

One evening, I was guided to watch the sun set. While the sun slowly made its descent and the moon gently appeared, taking its place in the sky, I heard the Voice of Guidance tell me:

There is a reason why some people do not get depressed by nightfall. They believe in the laws of the physical world in which the sun and the moon automatically exchange places every day, without any doubt (no worries).

In life, we symbolically associate the day with love and beauty, and the night with fear and pain. Actually, our darkness (our painful life experiences) is only temporary - the same as nature's day and night. This brings us the message of Hope, Peace, Joy, and Balance.

ROAD MAP:

1. Imagine the sun is slowly setting and you are looking forward to coming home after a day out. As you are getting close to home, the sun has set, daylight is leaving, and you are ready to spend some time relaxing and leaving the stress of the day behind in your thoughts.

2. Note that, now that the sun has gone down, you do not look out the window and say, "Where is the sun? Oh my gosh, the sun has abandoned me!" According to the laws of the physical world, as the earth rotates on its axis, giving us the day and night, you do not question the situation because you believe in the laws of science. And you do not blame the moon for taking away the sun and vice versa. This exemplifies how we should not judge any situation or experience, and we can see it as a lesson through duality every day of our lives.

3. Reflect on how choosing to awaken to the Truth, you see the sun and the moon showing you the lesson of Balance. When the sun sets, it is time to quiet down, relax, and go with the flow of night. You never struggle with the darkness of night, and you never ask, "Is tomorrow ever going to come? Will I ever see the sun (joy) again?"

This is the way you can look at the stress in illness. It is a quiet time to invite peace and hope into your space since we all have been disconnected from who we are. This is a time to return to the Peaceful spirit. You trust that no matter what, the sun will rise again in the morning (having hope, without question).

If there is darkness in your experience, it is only temporary because you have no doubts that the sun will return, and this is the same as knowing that no matter what, you are being taken care of at all times. Always remember that You never left the heart of God.

VIII. *Messages of the Falling Leaf*

Here is a tool from the Divine to help you quiet your mind, stay connected to the Source, and hear his Guidance. One morning, I was guided to look out the window when I saw a leaf lightly floating in the air. I knew that the leaf was instructing me to listen to the voice of God. I then heard his Loving voice say:

> **As you quiet your mind, you will hear my Guidance and you will feel my presence and my Love for You.**

Any time you notice a leaf falling, take a moment to be still and remember God to hear His messages.

ROAD MAP:

1. When you see a falling leaf, close your eyes to block out any distractions.
2. Now listen with your emotions to Divine guidance. This falling leaf has a message for you from God.
3. Feel grateful, while you are unwrapping His gift in the presence of the falling leaf, and thank Divine.

In practicing the tools we've covered, start with just one a day and be mindful to use it from the time you wake up until you go to sleep at night. After spending one full day on each method, you can repeat them as often as you would like. Your logical mind (the ego) may judge these tools. No matter what your logical mind is saying, tell yourself:

I am choosing peace, as I reclaim my Inner Power.
I am choosing freedom from the now, past and future.
And I am willing to start my life fresh as a newborn baby

I invite you to develop your own tools as you learn what works best for you. Most importantly, be sure to put these tools to use on a consistent basis, particularly as you face the exciting challenges of your day.

Practice Page

Practice Page

Twenty-Eight

MEDITATIONS FROM THE GROUP OF THE FATHER/MOTHERHOOD

Quiet your mind to hear the voice of God.

Since you have activated the tools by practicing them, you are now ready to experience the power of meditation with the Group of the Father/Motherhood. As the Group explained to me:

Guided meditation leads you to your Intuitive self (the voice of God) and to your imagination, which is where your True Power of co-creation lies. It also helps you experience and play in a whole new world of Reality by enabling you to:

- *Go within, not without;*
- *Feel the present moment;*
- *Be with You and reconnect to the Power within;*
- *Create with your Infinite imagination;*
- *Curb your desire to control or judge the present moment;*
- *Travel to the space of stillness;*

- *Quiet your mind to hear the voice of God;*
- *Reunite with Love, faith, and trust;*
- *Reach Inner Peace; and*
- *Let go and allow the Divine to come through and serve you with Love.*

In a meditative state, your fears will gradually quiet down with practice, and as the fear fades you will hear the gentle Voice of Love, not the voice of fear.

Your willingness to reach Infinite Love for one another will expand and build a bridge between Heaven and earth, inviting all of us to join in the heart of God (Oneness).

Just remember to be patient, as this will not happen overnight due to the fear and guilt that we are holding onto. Fear and guilt are neither the Voice of God nor the Truth. The Truth is Love and Peace. Therefore, meditation is the practice of getting to know who You truly are (the Power within).

You can meditate anytime, anywhere. There is no need to light a candle and sit with your legs crossed in a quiet room. Meditation can be practiced while you are talking, working out, shopping, doing the dishes, or mowing the lawn. There are no restrictions, except those that arise from your pulsing thoughts.

If any thoughts come, while you are meditating, tell them to sit quietly and you will take care of them in a few minutes. And thank them for their help and for reminding you of the things you need to tend to.

Divine Light

+ *Close your eyes and relax.*
+ *Take a deep breath.*
+ *Imagine your breath is the fuel to reach Divine Unconditional Love.*
+ *Allow this breath to take you to the space of Light.*
+ *The Light is here at this present moment to bring you Clarity once more.*
+ *Breathe in and breathe out.*
+ *As you are receiving this beautiful light of the Divine, breathe out and expand It to the whole world, the world of Wholeness.*
+ *As you are breathing in, your body is glowing with the unconditional light of the Divine.*
+ *Allow this light to soothe and to bring you total Peace.*
+ *Choose joy and choose stillness.*
+ *Allow your mind to release all of your thoughts.*
+ *Allow this loving light to clear your mind at this present moment.*
+ *Allow this light to lead you the way.*
+ *Breathe in and gain fuel to travel to the land of unconditional light, the light of the Divine.*
+ *As you are breathing out, allow this expansion to bring you the clarity of light.*
+ *Now as you are taking another breath, exhale and expand the light of the Divine.*
+ *This pure light is shining through your heart, the heart of God.*
+ *And so Love Is.*
+ *Take a deep breath and slowly come back to your beautiful self, as you are exhaling and expanding.*
+ *Wholeness Is here now.*

The Messages of Breath

✦ *Your breath is the connection between you and the Divine, the cord of* <u>*One*</u>*ness.*

✦ *The messages of breath will bring you Love and Peace.*

✦ *The messages of breath will bring you trust; like the trust you have in your breath.*

✦ *The messages of breath will bring you clarity.*

✦ *The messages of breath will take you home.*

✦ *The messages of breath will bring you stillness.*

✦ *The messages of breath will take you to the present moment, where unconditional Love resides, not time.*

✦ *As you are taking a deep breath, this breath is the cord and the remembrance of the connection between you and the Divine at all times.*

✦ *And always remember, the connection between you and the Divine is Eternal; He is always here.*

✦ *Allow God to bring His abundance and His beauty once more into your space, into your universe of* <u>*One*</u>*ness.*

✦ *God Is here now.*

Releasing and Trusting Meditation

This short meditation requires trust, faith, and stillness. There is no risk in practicing it because if you hand your pain and suffering to the Divine and then decide that you want it back, God will always honor your request. So you have nothing to lose. In addition, my Teachers shared that "your feelings and your body will tell you how many times you need to repeat the *meditation, depending on the severity of your stress."*

+ ***Close your eyes and take a deep breath.***
+ *Now imagine God is in your space.*
+ *Feel His presence and His nurturing Love.*
+ *Trust that He is here with you to take care of all of your stressful thoughts.*
+ **Take a deep breath.**
+ *As you exhale, put all of your worry thoughts on a serving tray and hand it to Him.*
+ *Trust that He is here to bring you Joy and Happiness.*
+ *Faith plays an important role here and now.*
+ *Ask God to take away your fear, and trust that there is nothing to be fearful about.*
+ *Trust that He will release it for you.*
+ ***Now take a deep breath.***
+ *As you are inhaling and exhaling, you feel the weight lift off your shoulders.*
+ *Be grateful for His presence and His nurturing Love.*
+ *Breathe and come back to your beautiful space of faith and trust.*
+ *As you are opening your eyes, feel the weightlessness of your spirit.*
+ *Now you feel free and peaceful.*
+ <u>One</u>ness Is Here Now.

The Garden Meditation

This meditation comes from my own experience. It is very quick, so this meditation is great to use when you are short on time, like during your lunch break.

+ *Sit outside in nature and look at a tree.*
+ *Now imagine the tree is extending its Love to you.*
+ *And the tree says:*
  - *"The only way you can feel my Love and appreciation for you is through your breath. Please inhale."*
  - *"As you are inhaling, I am giving you my Love."*
  - *"And as you are exhaling, with your willingness, you can offer your love back to me."*
+ *Repeat this and it will bring you Balance, Peace, and <u>Oneness</u> with all.*

Giving is like receiving and receiving is like giving. When we give to others without expecting anything in return, it provides us with a sense of fulfillment. And when we accept the gift that others are offering, we affirm their role within our shared community.

Fingertips Meditation

+ ***Take a deep breath.***
+ *Now stay with your breath.*
+ *As we are starting, bring your fingertips of both your hands together to form a pyramid and hold this position.*
+ ***Now take a deep breath.***
+ *Imagine your fingers are all of your helpers.*
+ *They are here at this present moment to welcome you to this beautiful attunement of Peace.*
+ ***Take a deep breath.***
+ *Now start with your thumbs.*
+ *Breathe in and pay attention to your thumbs.*
+ *Imagine your thumbs represent your Master Guides.*
+ *Welcome Them through your breath, the breath of Oneness.*
+ ***Breathe in and breathe out.***
+ *Next, focus on to the tips of your index fingers.*
+ *Your index fingers are your Angels, who are here to soothe you and to bring you Peace.*
+ ***Now breathe in and breathe out.***
+ *Your middle fingers, these are the Guides for Peace.*
+ *They are spreading Peace all around you, all around your heart.*
+ *Release and surrender to God's Love.*
+ *Trust.*
+ ***Now breathe in and breathe out.***
+ *Your ring fingers are your Hope Guides, and They are here at this present moment to be your servants.*
+ *Allow God's Light to shine through your mind.*
+ ***Breathe in and breathe out.***
+ *Pay attention to your pinky fingers.*
+ *These are You, Dear One.*
+ *You are here to be nurtured by your Guides.*
+ ***Breathe in and breathe out.***

✦ *Put your hands together in a prayer position.*

✦ *Feel the <u>Oneness</u> with your Angels.*

✦ *Know at this present moment that God is here as well.*

✦ *He is here to lead you to the land of <u>Oneness</u>.*

✦ *Trust and surrender to <u>Oneness</u> (God).*

✦ ***Breathe in and breathe out.***

✦ *Feel God's Love in your heart; He sees You as his little child, the little pinky that You are.*

✦ *Know that you are safe in the presence of God.*

✦ *Know that you are safe in the presence of the Angels.*

✦ *Know that you are safe in the presence of your Guides.*

✦ *Release all of your worries, all of your judgments, all of your discomfort to Them.*

✦ ***Take a deep breath.***

✦ *Allow this shower of Love, this shower of Abundance to come through your head, down to your knees, your legs, your toes, down to the ground.*

✦ *Wash away all of your doubts with God's Love.*

✦ *Know that you are not alone.*

✦ *Angels surround you at this present moment.*

✦ *Now take a deep breath and feel the <u>Oneness</u> with God and all within your hands.*

✦ *And with three deep, relaxed breaths, slowly open your eyes with the comfort of God.*

Experiences from the Meditation

Twenty-Nine

INCLUSION

---

*Just remember that becoming aware of emotions and
thoughts is a process . . . What does not feel familiar will
gradually guide you to unload your pain and distress,
see clearly, and lead you to the path that feels good.*

Inclusion = I + including God → <u>Oneness</u>

At this time, you have arrived at your *Universe* of Love. In the space of Love there are no questions or problems; there is nothing broken to fix. Even if it seems broken, you now have the tools to put the pieces back together and can see the whole picture (life lessons). In the loving mind, there is no confusion because love will melt anything. Knowing this, you can start your life innocent and pure as a newborn baby, with the mind of an Ancient and Infinite spirit.

Just remember that becoming aware of your emotions and thoughts is a process. You have to be patient and take baby steps. By being patient, present, and consistent, you can be trained to move through your life experiences with ease, as you are forever safe and being taken care of in the heart of God. If you only knew how loved, you are in His heart; He would never let anything hurt or destroy you.

Soon you will discover that He is constantly lavishing you with presents in the present moment. As you fearlessly unwrap His gifts, without any concerns or worries, know that whatever you are experiencing—whether it is good, bad, happy, or sad—will take you to the next step of empowerment and total wholeness. So even if you are going through pain and suffering, knowing the truth (of who You are) will guide you step by step to de-clutter your fearful thoughts in the light of the Divine. Just welcome your experiences with full trust in God, for each challenge will bring you to the point of simplicity (when you go to the center of your heart and feel the sense of completion with Him), where time and space no longer exist and are replaced with perfection.

In the Universe of Perfection, you value yourself and come to see that you are the King or Queen of your own universe. You are in charge of your emotions and thoughts. By realizing your true power within (knowing God), you will not allow your ego to knock you off your throne and tell you who to be, how to feel, where to go, and what to say.

Whenever you tell yourself fearful stories that bring you pain, go to The lab of emotions and feel the love versus the agony. Which story feels good? Which one is really draining you? The love that you feel is who you are and that is why it feels familiar, comfortable, and free of all judgment. What does not feel familiar will gradually guide you to unload your pain and distress, see clearly, and lead you to the path that feels good. It is no different than driving in an unknown area; you might feel nervous but you have the choice to stop, be patient, look at the map (awareness), and orient yourself on your own personal Expressway to Clarity.

On our journey together, you have mastered the language of the loving mind. And since you felt its vibration and heard the Source's guidance in your own heart, now you know how to reach the Truth of who You Truly are (Love). Be assured that Love speaks only in truth and in light, and the truth will lead you to the clarity of who God Is (Love).

Being that you have no fear of receiving Love, you can go with the flow and stay connected to the pulse of God's Loving mind. With His mind merging into yours, He will lift you to the state of total ecstasy and Peace. Here you are capable of projecting His Love onto You and All (<u>One</u>ness).

There is no beginning and no end to Divine Infinite Love for You.

~The Source wants YOU to know~

"My Love Is Whole and Complete with You.
I Am (<u>One</u>ness)."
Now put your hands together in a prayer position,
"My Beloved, as you are quieting Your mind. Feel the
<u>One</u>ness between You and Me within your hands.
Know that I AM always with You and shower-
ing You with Unconditional Love.
Take a deep breath and celebrate your new You and your new journey."

These awakening experiences and Divine guidance have helped me see the world through Eyes of the Source. I seek to empower us all and lead us to the flow of Eternal Love. I have witnessed entire stories of how other people arrived to their current state in life and discovered the underlying causes of their difficult situations. I have gathered knowledge from the Source to guide me in interpreting how to shift people's old, destructive beliefs and perceptions to achieve full consciousness and awareness.

Choose to see value in one another.
Life is complete because all of us are here together
like pieces of a puzzle.
Judge none and Love all.

Prayer

Tell yourself that Love Is.
There is nothing broken to fix.
I am Infinite.
I never left the Heart of God.
I am One with feeling good.
I am the Master of all Masters.
I am the King and the Queen
of my universe.

I am choosing Light at this present moment to
guide me through all darkness, and
through all life experiences.
And I trust in this Light to take me
to the Infinite Supply
of Divine Unconditional Love that
_I Am._
—Afie

About the Author

 fsaneh S. "Afie" Lattimer is a certified Reiki Master Practitioner, Teacher and physical guide who connects people to Divine Unconditional Love. She holds a degree in Health Science Education from the University of Florida, with a specialization in community health. Since childhood, the Divine has been communicating with and training Afie to serve as a guide between Heaven and Earth. Her life purpose became clear during a powerful near death experience, while undergoing childbirth, which changed her life. On the other side, she was presented with the choice to either remain there or return to finish her life's work in the physical world. Afie chose to return and spread the Source's Unconditional Love for us all.

Afie received guidance in 2000 to begin training in spirituality and Oneness guidance. She Afie was later guided to open The School of Oneness, which she launched in 2017. Also in that year, she was awarded for her popular class for cancer survivors and their caregivers which she teaches at the Hope Connections for Cancer Support in Bethesda, Maryland. She has shared over 400 tools and guided meditations to date during her weekly classes, workshops and talks, in addition to private sessions with clients from around the world.

To learn more about Afie's work and her spiritual journey, please visit www. AfieLattimer.com.

**Notes**

Notes

I hope you are enjoying your new universe and continue experimenting with the tools and meditations. Now that you've experienced simplicity and its lack of complications, you know that it is possible to be simple and to experience your life with playfulness and ease. Nothing is broken, and if it seems broken we will help you put the pieces back together to co-create and to experience the Perfection of God's Love.

Love Is.

To help you along your journey, please visit **www.AfieLattimer.com** and learn more about:

- The latest updates;
- School of Oneness
- The *Spiritual Lab* (aka empowerment workshops and retreats);
- Downloadable meditations;
- Publications;
- Videos;
- Speaking engagements;
- Individual; Group and couples';
- Private sessions; and
- Inner Peace and Healing class.

Just remember, you are never alone. God (Love) is
always holding your hands and guiding you to Eternal Light and Clarity!

AltarWithin, LLC
www.AfieLattimer.com

Made in the USA
Columbia, SC
11 February 2018